A Millennium of Turkish Literature

A Brave New Quest: 100 Modern Turkish Poems
   Talat S. Halman, trans. and ed.; Jayne L. Warner, assoc. ed.

*I, Anatolia and Other Plays: An Anthology of Modern
Turkish Drama, Volume Two*
   Talat S. Halman and Jayne L. Warner, eds.

*İbrahim the Mad and Other Plays: An Anthology of Modern
Turkish Drama, Volume One*
   Talat S. Halman and Jayne L. Warner, eds.

Nightingales and Pleasure Gardens: Turkish Love Poems
   Talat S. Halman, trans. and ed.; Jayne L. Warner, assoc. ed.

Popular Turkish Love Lyrics and Folk Legends
   Talat S. Halman; Jayne L. Warner, ed.

Rapture and Revolution: Essays on Turkish Literature
   Talat S. Halman; Jayne L. Warner, ed.

Sleeping in the Forest: Stories and Poems
   Sait Faik; Talat S. Halman, ed.; Jayne L. Warner, assoc. ed.

The Turkish Muse: Views and Reviews, 1960s–1990s
   Talat S. Halman; Jayne L. Warner, ed.

A Millennium
of
Turkish Literature

A CONCISE HISTORY

TALAT S. HALMAN

Edited by
Jayne L. Warner

Syracuse University Press

First Edition, Republic of Turkey Ministry of Culture and Tourism 2008
Revised Edition, Syracuse University Press 2011

11 12 13 14 15 16   6 5 4 3 2 1

∞ The paper used in this publication meets the minimum requirements
of the American National Standard for Information Sciences—Permanence
of Paper for Printed Library Materials, ANSI Z39.48-1992.

For a listing of books published and distributed by Syracuse University Press,
visit our Web site at SyracuseUniversityPress.syr.edu.

ISBN: 978-0-8156-0958-2

Library of Congress Cataloging-in-Publication Data

Halman, Talât Sait.
    A millennium of Turkish literature : a concise history / Talat S. Halman ;
edited by Jayne L. Warner. — Rev. ed.
        p. cm.
    Includes bibliographical references and index.
    ISBN 978-0-8156-0958-2 (pbk. : alk. paper)
    1. Turkish literature—History and criticism.   I. Warner, Jayne L.   II. Title.
    PL205.H345 2010
    894'.35—dc22   2010038681

Manufactured in the United States of America

CONTENTS

A Time-Honored Literature

TALAT S. HALMAN

F ROM ORHON INSCRIPTIONS TO ORHAN PAMUK: that could serve as a definition of the life story of Turkish literature from the eighth century A.D. to the present day. A geographic span from Outer Mongolia and the environs of China through Inner Asia, the Caucasus, the Middle East and North Africa, the Balkans and Europe all the way to North America. An amalgam of cultural and literary orientations that has embraced such traditions and influences as Chinese, Indian, Turkic, Mongolian, Uyghur, Russian, Arabo-Persian, Islamic, Sufi, Judaeo-Christian, Greek, Mesopotamian, Roman, Byzantine, European and Mediterranean, Scandinavian, Germanic and British, French and Spanish, North American, and Latin American.

Always receptive to the nurturing values, aesthetic tastes, and literary penchants from diverse civilizations, Turkish culture succeeded in evolving a sui generis personality. It clung to its own established traits, yet it was flexible enough to welcome innovations—or even revolutionary change.

Among living literatures that preceded Turkish literature, one can cite the Hebrew, Chinese, Greek, Arabic, Persian, German, Indian, Irish, Spanish, and perhaps two or three others.

Literature, the premier genre of Turkish culture, had its dawn in Mongolia's Orhon Valley, where in the 720s and 730s the Köktürks erected stelae featuring their historical narratives. These inscriptions still stand in situ. They relate the Köktürk experiences of conflict, defeat, and regained sovereignty. In moving terms, they emphasize the importance of cultural authenticity and of a quasi-national consciousness.

Turkic poetry made its debut in the Uyghur dialect presumably in the sixth century, although it is difficult to ascertain the exact date. By the tenth century, it had become a living tradition.

The *Dede Korkut* tales *(The Book of Dede Korkut),* often characterized as "the Turkish national epic," probably had their origins in the tenth century, although the epic took about another five centuries to make its transition from the oral tradition to its first written version.

It was in the second half of the eleventh century that two early major literary works, *Kutadgu Bilig (Wisdom of Royal Glory)* and *Divanü Lügâti't Türk* (Compendium and Lexicon of Turkish), made their advent. If one disregards all the preceding works (inscriptions, lyric poetry, myths, tales, etc.), these two substantial books mark the outset of Turkish literature.

The story of Turkish literature from the eleventh century to the twenty-first is rich and complex, full of firm traditions and daring transformations. It straddles the creative endeavors of small states, tribal communities, and principalities; a major state such as the Selçuk, the expansive and enduring Ottoman Empire, the modern Turkish Republic, and the newly independent Cypriot Turkish and Central Asian Turkic republics.

This literature achieved an impressive élan with the work of the humanistic mystic folk poet Yunus Emre, who lived in the late thirteenth and early fourteenth centuries. Ottoman literary creativity matured in the fifteenth century and produced its best works until the end of the eighteenth century. In the classical age of Ottoman culture, the urban elite distinguished itself with its prolific corpus of formal lyrics that dealt with empyreal themes but without ignoring real life. Although verse was regarded as intrinsically superior to prose, numerous prose works, principally the ten-volume *Seyahatname* (Book of Travels) by Evliya Çelebi in the seventeenth century, achieved an enduring place of pride.

As the power of the Ottoman Empire waned, intellectuals and writers engaged in a dynamic search for Western aesthetics, genres, and techniques. In the second half of the nineteenth century, European-type fiction, drama, criticism, and newspaper writing gained popularity. As a consequence, Turkish literature embraced Europeanization.

With the establishment of the Turkish Republic in 1923, modern literature gained ascendancy. The leftist poet-playwright Nazım Hikmet revolutionized Turkish poetry and attained to world-class stature. The female novelist Halide Edib (Adıvar) made an impact with her works, some of which she wrote in English and published in England and the United States. The genre of fiction was dominated in the second half of the twentieth century by Yaşar Kemal, whose prolific output came close to securing a Nobel Prize for him. That honor ultimately was won by a stimulating younger novelist, Orhan Pamuk, in 2006, the first Nobel ever for a Turk in any field. It stands as the culmination of a nation's passion for literature through many centuries and heralds future triumphs for Turkish poets, playwrights, essayists, and critics as well as for fiction writers.

This book tells the story of how those genres evolved and grew in stature on the Turkish mainland in the course of a thousand years. It stands as the first short history of that literature. It ineluctably glosses over many themes and leaves out innumerable authors and titles but strives to provide a balanced view, if not a comprehensive panorama, of a literature that has always served as a faithful mirror of a time-honored nation's culture.

The poems and excerpts have been translated by Talat S. Halman unless otherwise indicated. Portions of the author's earlier publications have been incorporated in this volume.

The author is grateful to Dr. Jayne L. Warner, a longtime colleague and collaborator, for her excellent editing. Thanks also go to Demet Güzelsoy Chafra, Öykü Terzioğlu, and Ceyda Akpolat for their help.

NOTE ON TURKISH
SPELLING AND NAMES

For Turkish authors, place-names, publications, and special terms, this volume employs modern Turkish spelling. The entries in Suggested Reading and the index are arranged according to the modern Turkish alphabet that appears below.

a	(like *gun*) var. *â* (like *are*)	m	(as in English)
b	(as in English)	n	(as in English)
c	(like *jade*)	o	(like *eau* in French)
ç	(*ch* of *chin*)	ö	(like *bird* or French *deux*)
d	(as in English)	p	(as in English)
e	(like *pen*)	r	(*r* of *rust*)
f	(as in English)	s	(*s* of *sun*)
g	(*g* of *good*)	ş	(*sh* of *shine*)
ğ	(makes preceding vowel longer)	t	(as in English)
h	(*h* of *half*)	u	(like *pull*) var. *û* (like *pool*)
ı	(like second vowel of *portable*)	ü	(like *tu* in French)
i	(like *it*) var. *î* (like *eat*)	v	(as in English)
j	(like *measure*)	y	(*y* of *you*)
k	(*k* of *king*)	z	(as in English)
l	(as in English)		

Exceptions include words that have become common in English and appear in English dictionaries in anglicized forms. Proper names have been kept in modern Turkish with two major exceptions—the names İstanbul and Izmir have been rendered with normal English spelling using *I* rather than *İ* unless they are part of a title.

Considerable confusion persists in the spelling and forms of transliteration of earlier words, terms, and names. For centuries before and during the entirety of the Ottoman Empire, the Turkish language, which had an extensive vocabulary borrowed from Arabic and Persian, employed the Arabic script.

The Turkish Republic, established in 1923, changed the orthography to a Latin typescript in 1928. Because no coherent system of spelling was created at the time of the transition from the Arabic to the Latin alphabet, extensive and frequent adjustments were made and continue to be made. The editor cautions that spelling variations persist. One example is the terminal *d* found in many prerepublican names. Some of the same or similar names appear with a terminal *t* in recent decades.

To complicate matters, surnames were legally introduced with the passage of the Surname Law by the Turkish Republic in 1934. As a consequence, scores of authors and scholars whose prior publications had come out without surnames began to appear in reference books, bibliographical entries, and on title pages with official surnames after 1934.

All these variations are reflected in this book as well, although certain proper names have been standardized. Sait Faik took the last name Abasıyanık following the passage of the Surname Law, but he virtually never used it for his books; therefore, the name Sait Faik has been maintained here. Orhan Veli Kanık, however, frequently used his surname, and although he is often simply referred to as Orhan Veli, his full name is given. Nazım Hikmet used his official surname, Ran, so infrequently that it is not even given in this history. Ahmet Muhip Dranas inserted an *ı* in his surname late in his life; it is that spelling (Dıranas) that appears here. The modern Turkish spelling of the name Mevlana Celaleddin Rumi has been employed throughout.

A Millennium of Turkish Literature

The Dawn in Asia

TURKISH LITERATURE is among the world's oldest—and youngest—literatures. Its creative tradition, according to some debatable claims made by numerous scholars, dates back to before Christ. It is commonly accepted, however, that its legacy of written works spans twelve centuries.[1]

In their long history, the Turks have gone through more changes than most nations, and yet—paradoxical as it may sound—they have preserved most of their basic cultural traits. Through the centuries, they lived as nomadic tribes, built small and large states in parts of Asia, created the Selçuk state in Asia Minor and later the sprawling Ottoman Empire, which endured from the thirteenth to the early twentieth century, and finally established the modern Turkish Republic. At different stages of their history, Turkic communities embraced shamanism, Buddhism, Judaism, Christianity, Manichaeanism, Zoroastrianism, and other creeds until most of them accepted the Islamic faith more than a thousand years ago. Their language, one of the world's most regular in grammar and also one of the most agglutinative, has used five separate scripts: Köktürk, Uyghur, Arabic, Cyrillic, and (since 1928) one based on the Latin alphabet.

The pattern of the main ages of Turkish literature follows the foregoing outline of the major periods of Turkish history. But scholars have pursued a variety of approaches to the periodization of Turkish literary

---

1. A useful and reliable general history of Turkish literature is Talat S. Halman, gen. ed., *Türk Edebiyatı Tarihi,* 4 vols. (Ankara: T. C. Kültür ve Turizm Bakanlığı, 2006; 2d ed., 2007).

 5-stage theory

development. The simplest approach sets up two stages: early (eighth to nineteenth century) and modern (nineteenth to twenty-first century). Another breakdown involves three periods: pre-Islamic (until the eleventh century), Islamic (eleventh to mid–nineteenth century), and modern (mid–nineteenth century to the present). A different three-pronged categorization is: pre-Ottoman (until the thirteenth century), Ottoman (thirteenth to twentieth century), and twentieth century to the present. A more elaborate—also more meaningful—approach sets up five stages: pre-Islamic (until the eleventh century), pre-Ottoman Islamic (eleventh to thirteenth century), Ottoman (thirteenth to mid–nineteenth century), transitional (mid–nineteenth century to the 1920s), and modern (1920s to the present). All these periods have their subdivisions, on which, however, there is no unanimity among literary historians.

Few cultures have changed as drastically and still remained as intact as has Turkish culture throughout history. Turkish history has included "some cataclysmic transformations in terms of locale, cultural orientation, faith, system of government, allegiance."[2] Language is a particularly compelling example of transformation and continuity. From the tenth to the twentieth century, Turkish intellectuals and men of letters voraciously absorbed Persian and Arabic vocabulary as well as some of the grammatical devices of these two languages. Yet despite the elitist enthusiasm for such borrowings, the language spoken by the masses remained remarkably unchanged and was preserved not only in colloquial use from generation to generation, but also in folk literature. As a result, in terms of morphology, syntax, and a substantial portion of vocabulary, the Turkish language is essentially the same as it was a thousand years ago.[3]

"Man's legacy to man is words. . . . Whosoever is born must die, but his words live on. Language is the interpreter of thought and science. It gives man dignity. Human beings attain happiness through language. But language can also demean man and cause heads to roll. It is on words that man

2. Talat S. Halman, "Poetry and Society: Propaganda Functions of Poetry in the Turkish Experience," in Talat S. Halman, *Rapture and Revolution: Essays on Turkish Literature*, edited by Jayne L. Warner (Syracuse, N.Y.: Syracuse Univ. Press, 2007), 159.

3. A comprehensive survey of language reform is Uriel Heyd, *Language Reform in Modern Turkey* (Jerusalem: Israel Oriental Society, 1954). Also see Geoffrey Lewis, *The Turkish Language Reform: A Catastrophic Success* (Oxford, U.K.: Oxford Univ. Press, 1999).

can rise and acquire power and prestige."[4] Yusuf Has Hâcib of the eleventh century, the first Turkish poet to produce a major original work, *Kutadgu Bilig (Wisdom of Royal Glory),* proclaimed in these words the supremacy of language in Turkish life and culture. Throughout the later stages of Turkish history and most significantly during the Ottoman period, the poetic word was a more prevalent method of expression than most other modes. Today, too, the spoken and written word is the pivotal force of Turkish culture.

Because the Turks originated in the Ural-Altai region of Central Asia, their language is often referred to as "Ural-Altaic," together with such other Turkic languages as Uzbek, Azeri, Chaghatai, Kirghiz, and Yakut. It is an agglutinative language rich in rhythmic effects and rhyme potential, with a mellifluous phonological structure ideally suited for poetic utterance.

It is, however, with the Orhon inscriptions of the eighth century A.D.[5] that we get the most significant documents of early Turkish literature. These inscriptions as well as the oral epics[6] and a large body of oral lyric verse[7] constitute the best work of the nomadic and settled Turkish communities until the latter part of the eleventh century.

Thus, the Turkish migration that started around the sixth century A.D.—a migration into China, India, Persia, the Caucasus, and Asia Minor—brought with it a rich oral tradition. Between the ninth and early thirteenth centuries, a vast majority of the Turks who settled in Asia Minor

4. Yusuf Has Hâcib, *Kutadgu Bilig,* 2 vols., edited by Reşit Rahmeti Arat (vol. 1, Ankara: Milli Eğitim, 1947; vol. 2, Ankara: Türk Tarih Kurumu, 1959), 1:33–35, 2:23–24. For an English translation of *Kutadgu Bilig,* see Yusuf Khass Hajib, *Wisdom of Royal Glory: A Turko-Islamic Mirror for Princes,* edited and translated by Robert Dankoff (Chicago: Univ. of Chicago Press, 1983).

5. The best work on the inscriptions was done by the Russian Turkologist Wilhelm Radloff and the Danish linguist Vilhelm Thomsen. The earliest comprehensive Turkish work on them is Hüseyin Namık Orkun, *Eski Türk Yazıtları* (Istanbul: Devlet, 1936; reprint, Ankara: Türk Tarih Kurumu, 1986). Also see the excellent scholarly works by Talat Tekin, *A Grammar of Orkhon Turkic* (Bloomington: Indiana Univ. Press, 1968) and *Orhon Yazıtları* (Istanbul: Simurg, 1989).

6. For a comprehensive study, see Nora K. Chadwick and Victor Zhirmunsky, *Oral Epics of Central Asia* (London: Cambridge Univ. Press, 1969).

7. A large selection of early Turkish poems may be found in Reşit Rahmeti Arat, *Eski Türk Şiiri* (Ankara: Türk Tarih Kurumu, 1965), and Saadet Çağatay, *Türk Lehçeleri Örnekleri* (Ankara: Türk Tarih Kurumu, 1950).

accepted Islam as their faith. By the end of the eleventh century, much of Turkish literature, oral and written, had already acquired an Islamic flavor. This orientation, together with the influence of Arabic and Persian cultures, was to continue throughout Ottoman history.

In addition to the early *Dede Korkut* tales, which recount the Turks' heroic exploits, the oral tradition produced a large body of legends and stories. This tradition's principal achievement is folk poetry composed by minstrels and troubadours, who voiced in a spontaneous, sincere, and simple language the sensibilities, yearnings, social protests, and critical views of the uneducated classes. Utilizing Turkic verse forms and syllabic meters, often extemporized and sung to musical accompaniment and replete with assonances, alliterations, and inexact rhymes, folk poetry harped on the themes of love, heroism, the beauties of nature, and, at times, mysticism.

The epic and lyric traditions among ancient Turks probably emerged in Central Asia. Some of the earliest specimens of verse attributed to Turks are available only in Chinese translation. These epigrammatic poems (possibly excerpts) reveal a refined and subtle poetic sense:[8]

> Young girls are weaving cloth,
> I can't hear the sound of the loom,
> But I hear those girls breathing.

In Uyghur texts, we find many early verses, some attributed to individual poets, others anonymous, but many were accomplished practitioners of their art, as can be seen in the closing stanzas of the prince Aprin Çor Tigin's "Love Poem":

> Gods of light, grant me this bliss
> Let my soft gentle darling and I
> Join our lives forever.
>
> Mighty angels, give us power
> So that my black-eyed sweetheart and I
> Can live and laugh together.

---

8. For specimens of earliest Turkish verses in Chinese sources, see Muhaddere N. Özerdim, "Çin'in Şimalinde Hanedan Kuran Türklerin Şiirleri," *Ankara Üniversitesi Dil ve Tarih-Coğrafya Fakültesi Dergisi*, no. 1 (1943): 89–98.

In settled communities and among the nomadic tribes alike, the epics and song lyrics served as a principal vehicle of aesthetic experience and communal solidarity. Although all but one of the long epics, the *Oğuzname,* failed to survive intact, the material that has come down to the present in partial or fragmentary form charts the continuity of literary evolution while presenting a panorama of life and culture among the Turks before their conversion to Islam.

The early epics are usually poetically conceived depictions of gods and heroes. Among them we find a fairly elaborate cosmogony, mythic accounts of the emergence of the Turks, stories about preternatural phenomena, and many legends of victory and defeat, migration and catastrophe.

Epic literature evolved as a collective creative endeavor and was kept alive, with substantial changes over the centuries, by minstrels—often called *ozan*s or sometimes *bahşi*s—who, accompanying themselves on a stringed instrument commonly referred to as a *kopuz,* narrated stories and chanted poems.[9]

The legend of creation, perhaps the earliest of Turkish legends, traces the origin of the universe to a single creator, the god Kara Han, who finds his inspiration in the appearance of White Mother's face emerging out of water. Kara Han's first creature is man, who attempts to soar higher than his creator. Man is therefore deprived of the power to fly and remains condemned to earthbound life. The devil is shown in the legend as stronger than man but powerless before God.

The early Turks had animistic and pagan forms of worship. Shamanism held sway in many communities. Most of the moral themes in pre-Islamic Turkish legends appear as metaphors that seek to contrast good and evil. The dominant view is anthropomorphic.

The *Ergenekon* epic, an extended version of the popular *Bozkurt* (Gray Wolf) legend, is a picaresque depiction of a major Turkish community that escapes extinction thanks to the procreation and protection of its

9. For early Turkish literature, the most reliable source is the work of Mehmed Fuad Köprülü, principally *Türk Edebiyatında İlk Mutasavvıflar* (Ankara: Ankara Üniversitesi Basımevi, 1966; reprint, Ankara: Türk Tarih Kurumu, 1976); *Türk Edebiyatı Tarihi* (Istanbul: Matbaa, 1926); *Edebiyat Araştırmaları* (Ankara: Türk Tarih Kurumu, 1966); and "Turks: B: III–Ottoman Turkish Literature," in *Encyclopaedia of Islam* (Leiden and London: Brill and Luzac, 1913), 4:938–59.

totem-god Gray Wolf. A tale of survival, *Ergenekon* culminates in the story of how the Turks, incarcerated in a death valley surrounded by mountains that give no passage, dig a tunnel through an ironclad mountain and escape from the valley with Gray Wolf's guidance.

Among the oldest specimens of written literary works are memorial tablets, stone monoliths, and stelae found in the Yenisei Valley of northeastern Mongolia as well as documents unearthed in the Sinkiang region of modern China. Dating from the seventh to the ninth century, these works include stories of the battles the Turks fought against the Chinese, a variety of legends, and numerous specimens of verse (found mostly in Chinese translation) written in Uyghur Turkish.

The epic literature that evolved in the Uyghur period is a narration of the emergence of tribes, their peripatetic adventures, their fight for survival against natural disasters and hostile communities, of exodus and injustice, of brave deeds and social disintegration, of victory and enslavement.

The only long epic from this period that remains intact is the *Oğuz* epic, whose origin might conceivably go as far back as twenty centuries. It is an elaborate and lyrical description of superhuman and worldly episodes in the life of the legendary hero Oğuz. The focal themes are heroism and the struggle for survival. In blending miracles with daily life, the epic utilizes the motifs of nature's power and beauty. Interspersed in it are lyric passages that are further proof that ancient Turkic verse, in substance and form, had by this early period attained an appreciable level of artistry.

Early Turkish communities produced many poems for different social and ritual occasions. It was customary to chant poems at quasi-religious ceremonies held before the hunt *(sığır)* and at the festivities after the hunt *(şölen)*. Poetry was a vital ingredient of funerals and memorial services *(yuğ)*, where elegies called *sagu* were recited. Poems of joy and love were featured on festive occasions. The lyrics of the songs offered as part of communal entertainment represented a major segment of the poetic lore.

In the pre-Islamic era, Turks composed their verses in indigenous quantitative meters, which were based on an identical number of syllables, with one or two caesurae to a line. The stanzaic form, usually in units of four lines, relied heavily on rhyming, the most frequent pattern being *abab / cccb / dddb*. In some of the early poems, rhymes appeared not at the end of lines, but at the beginning.

The lyric and epic traditions of the early centuries led to the master-works of the pre-Ottoman period: *Divanü Lügâti't Türk,* an encyclopedic compendium of Turkish linguistics and poetry; *Kutadgu Bilig,* a mirror for princes; and Yunus Emre's mystic folk poetry, which is notable for, among other things, its universalist humanism.

Some fine accomplishments of early Turkish poetry have been preserved in the comprehensive survey of Turkic languages compiled under the title *Divanü Lügâti't Türk* by Kâşgarlı Mahmud in the late eleventh century. This first work of "national cultural consciousness" contains many lyrics of love and sorrow, as well as of hero worship and lament:

> Is Alp Er Tunga dead and gone
> While the evil world lives on?
> Has time's vengeance begun?
> Now hearts are torn to shreds.

In the *Divanü Lügâti't Türk,* Kâşgarlı Mahmud, whose birth one thousand years ago was celebrated in 2008, cited a probably apocryphal hadith (traditional saying attributed to Prophet Muhammad) conferring God's blessing on the Turks' military and political power: "God Almighty said: 'I have an army to which I gave the name *Turk.* I had the Turks settle in the East. Whenever a nation displeases me, I send the Turks against that nation.'" Mahmud also made the statement: "Learn Turkish, for Turkish sultans will rule for many years to come."[10]

The writing of the *Kutadgu Bilig* by Yusuf Has Hâcib coincided almost exactly with that of the *Divanü Lügâti't Türk.* Yet these two works could not be more disparate in orientation: the *Divan,* although written mostly in Arabic, is quintessentially "Turkish," whereas the *Kutadgu Bilig*—a monumental philosophical treatise in verse (approximately 6,500 couplets) on government, justice, and ethics—reflects the author's assimilation of Islamic concepts, of Arabic and Persian culture, including its orthography, vocabulary, and prosody.

This disparity was to become the gulf that divided Turkish literature well into the twentieth century—the gulf, namely, between *poesia d'arte*

---

10. Kâşgarlı Mahmud, *Divan ü Lûgat-it-Türk,* 5 vols., edited by Besim Atalay (Ankara: Türk Dil Kurumu, 1939–43).

and *poesia popolare,* to use Benedetto Croce's two categories. The first embodies elite, learned, ornate, refined literature; the second represents spontaneous, indigenous, down-to-earth, unassuming oral literature. *Poesia d'arte* is almost always an urban phenomenon, whereas *poesia popolare* usually flourishes in the countryside. The former, as the name suggests, has a strong commitment to the principle of "art for art's sake," whereas the latter is preponderantly *engagé* or utilitarian in function and substance.

In the two centuries prior to the establishment of the Ottoman state, while the process of Islamization gained momentum, the intellectual elite of the Anatolian Turkish states produced Islamic treatises, poems, translations, and Koranic commentaries. In the second half of the twelfth century, the *Divan-ı Hikmet* (Poems of Wisdom) by Ahmet Yesevi, founder of a principal mystic sect, and the *Atebet-ül Hakayık* (The Threshold of Truths), a long poetic tract by Edib Ahmed about ways of achieving moral excellence, wielded wide religious and literary influence. The Turkish legends, principally the *Oğuz* epic and in particular the *Dede Korkut* tales,[11] which antedated the conversion to Islam, acquired a distinctly Islamic flavor. *The Book of Dede Korkut,* composed of twelve legends, narrates in prose and verse the adventures of the Oğuz Turks migrating from Central Asia to Asia Minor. These tales of heroism constitute the Turks' principal national epic, which invites comparison with the world's best epic literature. Although the martial spirit dominates *The Book of Dede Korkut,* it also has eloquent passages that express a yearning for peace and tranquility:

> If the black mountains lying out there were quite safe,
> Then people would go there to live.
> If the rivers whose waters flow bloody were safe,
> They would all flood their banks for joy.
> If black stallions were safe,
> They would then sire colts,
> If the camel were safe in the midst of the herd,
> She would mother young camels there.

11. The *Dede Korkut* tales appear in two English translations: *The Book of Dede Korkut: A Turkish Epic,* edited and translated by Faruk Sümer, Ahmet E. Uysal, and Warren S. Walker (Austin: Univ. of Texas Press, 1972), and *The Book of Dede Korkut,* translated by Geoffrey Lewis (Harmondsworth, U.K.: Penguin, 1974).

If the white sheep were safe in the fold,
She would bear there her lambs,
And if gallant princes were safe,
They would all be the fathers of sons.

> (Translated by Faruk Sümer, Ahmet E. Uysal,
> and Warren S. Walker)[12]

The earliest identifiably Turkic groups of Central Asia were settled communities with a distinctive culture and oral literary tradition. Most of them became peripatetic tribes after leaving their homeland under the pressure of natural hardships (perhaps droughts or floods) or marauding enemies. Some resettled in nearby regions, others moved on to the distant Far East or the Near East. The exodus brought them in contact with diverse cultures and communities, from which they acquired tools and terms, concepts and concrete objects—thus indicating their receptivity to anything useful that would serve their purposes.

The individual and the conglomerate nomadic tribes migrating into Anatolia—engaging in combat on the way, intermingling with other people, carrying their values of survival and mobility—evolved into principalities, into small and major states until the end of the thirteenth century. They conquered Baghdad in 1055 and gained control of Anatolia in 1071 as a result of the victory at Manzikert against the emperor of Byzantium. The Turkish Selçuk state emerged with a high culture of its own—affluent, excelling in theology and the arts.[13]

It was not an accident of history that most of the fighting Turks of a millennium ago bypassed Judaism and Christianity, with which they had come into close contact in Asia Minor. Islam's appeal to them was manifold. In Geoffrey Lewis's words, "The demands which it makes are few; the rewards which it promises are great, particularly to those who die battling 'in the Path of Allah.' But what must have had even more weight with the

12. *The Book of Dede Korkut: A Turkish Epic,* edited and translated by Faruk Sümer, Ahmet E. Uysal, and Warren S. Walker (Austin: Univ. of Texas Press, 1972), 83.

13. For the Selçuk period, see Claude Cahen, *Pre-Ottoman Turkey,* translated by J. Jones-Williams (New York: Taplinger, 1968); Osman Turan, *Selçuklular Tarihi ve Türk-İslam Medeniyeti* (Ankara: Türk Kültürünü Araştırma Enstitüsü, 1965); and various publications by Mehmet Altay Köymen.

Turks who came over to Islam in such numbers during the tenth century was the fact that acceptance of Islam automatically conferred citizen-rights in a vast and flourishing civilization."[14] Once conversion to Islam became firmly entrenched, the Turks started serving the cause of Muslim domination and *propaganda fide*. As Julius Germanus has observed, "Islam and its martial spirit was one of the greatest motives in the uninterrupted success of the Turks. They had fought, as idolaters before, for the sake of rapine and glory, but the propagation of the faith gave a moral aim to their valor and enhanced their fighting quality."[15] In time, Islam became so pervasive a force that the Ottomans ceased to consider themselves Turks, proudly identifying themselves as Muslims.[16]

Dede Korkut *Tales*

The Book of Dede Korkut *has been called the* Iliad *of the Turks. The similarities are too few and too inconsequential to warrant systematic comparison, but, like the* Iliad, *the stories of Dede Korkut represent and embody the epic élan of a nation's literary imagination. Constructed not as a monolithic work but as a series of interrelated legends,* The Book of Dede Korkut *relates in prose and verse the tribulations of the Oğuz, an ancestral nomadic Turkish tribe, in their migration from Central Asia to parts of the Middle East. The stories that make up the epic have collective authorship in the form in which they were transcribed, although originally they may have been the work of a single writer. Since its emergence, possibly in the tenth century, the epic has undergone much substantive and stylistic change as a part of living oral literature. A significant aspect of its evolution was the introduction of Islamic themes as the Turks gradually adopted Islam.*

14. Geoffrey Lewis, *Turkey,* 3rd ed. (London: Benn, 1965), 21.

15. Julius Germanus, "The Role of the Turks in Islam," in *The Traditional Near East,* edited by J. Stewart-Robinson (Englewood Cliffs, N.J.: Prentice-Hall, 1966), 100–101.

16. Bernard Lewis, *The Emergence of Modern Turkey* (London: Oxford Univ. Press, 1966; 3rd ed., 2002), 2.

Selçuk Sufism

TURKISH COMMUNITIES, through many centuries, experienced the duality of the *gazi* (warrior, conquering hero) and Sufi (mystic) spirits. Whereas the raiders and the soldiers of Islam kept waging war to expand the frontiers of the faith, the Sufis—men of peace, humanism, and love—preached the virtues of tranquility in the heart and all over the world. The mystic philosopher whose thoughts and spiritual guidance were to dominate Anatolia from the thirteenth century onward and to inspire many nations in modern times was Mevlana Celaleddin Rumi (1207–73). With his poetic celebrations of love and the arts and life itself, he heralded in the thirteenth century a new glittering age of humanistic mysticism. His ideas—which stressed the deathlessness of the loving soul, the joys of passion, the inherent worth of the human being, the aesthetic and ecstatic imperative of faith, the need to go beyond the confines of scholasticism and to transcend schisms, and, above all, the godliness of man—not only gave renewed vigor to Islamic mysticism, but also represented for the Islamic religion in general a counterpart of the Renaissance, which was to emerge in Europe a century after Rumi's death.

Recognition of Rumi's enduring moral force in the Islamic world and his intellectual impact elsewhere has prompted many prominent figures to praise him. The British Orientalist Reynold A. Nicholson, an indefatigable translator of Rumi's verse, paid tribute to him as "the greatest mystical poet of any age." For his *Westöstlicher Divan,* Goethe drew inspiration from some of Rumi's poems translated into German. One of the immortals of Persian classical poetry, Jami (d. 1492), said of him: "He is not a prophet, but he has written a holy book," referring to the *Mesnevi* (Persian original: *Mathnawi*), which has also been called "The Koran of Mysticism" and "The Inner Truth of the Koran." Gandhi used to quote his couplet "To unite—that is why we came / To divide—that is not our aim." UNESCO's first director-general, Julian Huxley, lauded Rumi's spirit of international brotherhood. In 1958, Pope John XXIII wrote a special message: "In the name of the Catholic world, I bow with respect before the memory of Mevlana." On the philosophic value of his poetry, Hegel saw him as one of the great poets and thinkers in world history. At the close of his *Encyclopaedia,* in approaching God as Absolute Mind, Hegel cites the "excellent" Celaleddin Rumi at length, saying that "if we want to see the consciousness of the One . . . in its finest purity and sublimity," we cannot do better than to read that mystic's verses. The unity with the One, in love, set forth there is, Hegel concludes, "an exaltation above the finite and vulgar, a transfiguration of the natural and the spiritual, in which the externalism and transitoriness of immediate nature, and of empirical secular spirit, is discarded and absorbed."

Celaleddin was born in Balkh (in present-day Afghanistan) in 1207, the son of a renowned scholar and mystic, Bahaüddin Veled. When Celaleddin was about twelve years old, his family was forced to flee Balkh probably either because of an impending Mongol onslaught or the result of an intellectual-political disagreement between Bahaüddin and the sultan. The family wandered through Persia and the Arab lands for ten years without finding a city receptive to Bahaüddin's independent spirit and unorthodox ideas. Finally, the city of Konya welcomed them. Celaleddin was twenty-two years old when they arrived in Konya, which had been a Selçuk city for nearly 150 years. The capital of the Turkish Selçuk Empire, it was a center of high culture and enjoyed a climate of tolerance and freedom. Although predominantly Turkish and Muslim, Rumi's new home had a cosmopolitan population with Christian, Jewish, Greek, and Armenian communities. Islamic sects and non-Muslim communities coexisted and flourished. He lived there until his death on December 17, 1273, at the age of sixty-six. The city afforded him the atmosphere and the opportunity to evolve and express his new ideas, which included cultural values from the diverse religions and sects active in the Selçuk capital. He achieved distinction as a young theologian and Sufi. It was in Konya that Rumi's philosophy engendered the Mevlevi movement or sect (which has come to be known in the West as "The Whirling Dervishes").

In 1244, a dramatic encounter changed Mevlana's spiritual life. In Konya, he met a wild mystic who seemed to have come out of nowhere—Şems of Tabriz. It is said that Rumi discovered the inner secrets of love through

Şems's influence and came to the realization that love transcends the mind. At this stage in his life, at age thirty-seven, he was above all a scholar. He had read in depth in Persian, Arabic, Turkish, Greek, and Hebrew and commanded vast encyclopedic knowledge. But now passion reigned supreme over his mind. The frontiers of the intellect suddenly appeared too narrow, constricting, claustrophobic.

As a result of his affection, perhaps love, for Şems, he embarked on a period of virtually constant ecstasy and excitement, of poetic creativity, of immersion in music—and the *sema,* mystic whirling.

The passions of the mystic mind that Mevlana called "my spiritual kingdom," intensified by his pains and ecstasies, gave rise to his collection of odes and quatrains entitled *Divan-ı Kebir* and to the great *Mesnevi,* consisting of some twenty-six thousand couplets, which is a masterwork of poetic narration and Sufi wisdom.

It is small wonder that the great mystic was given the supreme title "Mevlana" (Our Lord, Grand Master). His reputation rests not only on the spiritual heights he attained in his poetry, but also on his having brought the dimension of aesthetics to mysticism in a systematic and comprehensive way. Poetry, music, dance, and the visual arts—rare in most Islamic movements—were integrally combined in the practices of the Mevlevi Order. Not only the synesthesia of the verbal, musical, and visual genres, but more comprehensively the unified use of intellectual, spiritual, and artistic elements constituted the hallmark of Mevlana's faith.

Rumi may well be the only major philosopher in history, after Lucretius, to express and formulate an entire system of thought in poetic form. Taken together, his *Mesnevi, Divan-ı Kebir,* and *Rubaiyat* represent perhaps the world's most resourceful synthesis of poetry and philosophy, conflating the lyric, narrative, epic, didactic, epigrammatic, satiric, and elegiac norms. They embody the aesthetics of ethics and metaphysics. His *Mesnevi* makes a monumental synthesis of mystic ideas ranging from Neoplatonism to Chinese thought, embracing Indian, Persian, and Greek mythology, stories from the holy books, as well as Arab and Persian legends and folk stories. Certainly, no mystic poet has surpassed him in the more than seven centuries since his death.

The mystic's predicament is that he or she has temporarily fallen apart from God's reality and beauty. The divine image, God's human manifestation, yearns to return to the beloved Godhead. The mystic feels a sublime love that remains unrequited until he suffers so intensely in his spiritual exile that he finally reaches the blissful state of the submergence of his self-hood, the death of his ego.

The time of attainment is celebrated in one of Rumi's most rhapsodical *rubai*s:

> This is such a day: the sun is dazzling twice as before
> A day beyond all days, unlike all others—say no more . . .
> Lovers, I have great news for you: from the heavens above
> This day of love brings songs and flowers in a downpour.

One of his most subtle *rubai*s evokes the mystery of spiritual elevation beyond the proverbial spring. But only a unique soul is capable of it—a single branch among all the trees:

> This season is not the spring, it is some other season.
> The languid trances in the eyes have a different reason,
> And there is another cause for the way each single branch
> Dallies by itself while all the trees sway in unison.

For Rumi, love is the paramount component of mystic theology:

> The religion of love is apart from all religions;
> The lovers of God have no religion but God alone.

Rumi felt little respect for organized religion and stressed the primacy of internal faith and inner allegiance:

> I roamed the lands of Christendom from end to end
> Searching all over, but He was not on the Cross.

> I went into the temples where the Indians worship idols
> And the Magians chant prayers to fire—I found no trace of Him.

> Riding at full speed, I looked all over the Kaaba
> But He was not at that sanctuary for young and old.

> Then I gazed right into my own heart:
> There, I saw Him . . . He was there and nowhere else.

Peace, in Rumi's view, is a focal virtue to be nurtured and defended for the individual and the community. In his lifetime, he witnessed the ravages of the Mongol invasion and the Crusades. World peace was a supreme ideal for him. He stood against injustice and tyranny: "When weapons and ignorance come together, pharaohs arise to devastate the world with their cruelty," an observation that still holds true more than seven hundred years after his death. One of his most eloquent couplets proclaims:

> Whatever you think of war, I am far, far from it;
> Whatever you think of love, I am that, only that, all that.

Rumi had a humanistic, universalist, humanitarian vision: "I am," he declared, "a temple for all mankind."

> Like a compass I stand firm with one leg on my faith
> And roam with the other leg all over the seventy-two nations.
>
> — — —
>
> Seventy-two nations hear of their secrets from us:
> We are the reed whose song unites all nations and faiths.

Proclaiming that "my faith and my nation are God," Rumi made a plea for universal brotherhood in a world torn asunder by conflicting ideologies, sectarian divisions, religious strife, and jingoistic nationalism. One of his universalist statements is remarkable for his time: "Hindus, Kipchaks, Anatolians, Ethiopians—they all lie peacefully in their graves, separately, yet the same color." The "Sultan of Lovers" also wrote one of the most eloquent lines of ecumenism:

> In all mosques, temples, churches I find one shrine alone.

From the twentieth century onward, Rumi's poetry gained international recognition thanks to extensive translation activity. Mevlevi ceremonies, too, earned passionate interest worldwide. In ballet, documentaries, music, literature, and scholarship, Rumi and the dervishes left their imprint. In 2007, the eight hundredth anniversary of Rumi's birth was celebrated in dozens of countries and at the United Nations and UNESCO.

Rumi is included in this survey despite the fact that he composed his vast poetic corpus in Persian (except for a smattering of verses in Arabic, Turkish, and other languages) because he lived and wrote in Konya in the heartland of Anatolia for almost two-thirds of his life and because his spirituality, mysticism, and poetics have exerted an encompassing and enduring impact on Turkish culture since the thirteenth century, starting with the prominent mystic folk poet Yunus Emre (d. ca. 1321).

By the late thirteenth century, Islamic mysticism, in particular Rumi's Sufi philosophy, had become influential in many parts of the new homeland of the Turks. After several centuries of turmoil in Anatolia—with the ravages of the Crusades, the Byzantine-Selçuk wars, the Mongol invasions, strife among various Anatolian states and principalities, and frequent secessionist uprisings still visible or continuing—there was a craving for peace based on an appreciation of man's inherent worth. Mysticism, which attributes godlike qualities to man, became the apostle of peace and the chief defender of man's value.

Hacı Bektaş Veli
(Thirteenth Century)

An influential Anatolian mystic who formulated compelling ethical precepts, Hacı Bektaş Veli was the founder of the Bektaşi sect, which was to become the most popular of Anatolian sects. His teachings continue to inspire the people of Turkey.

> —*"If a road is not traveled with knowledge and science, it leads you to darkness."*
> —*"Never forget that your enemy, too, is human."*
> —*"Do not hurt even if you are hurt."*
> —*"If you sow a heart, you will reap a heart."*
> —*"If you want to live proud and brave, be just above all."*
> —*"How happy is he who holds a torch to darkness."*

The tradition of Turkish humanism is best represented by Yunus Emre. His poetry embodies the quintessence of Turkish Anatolian–Islamic humanism. He was the most significant literary figure of Turkish Anatolia to assimilate the teachings of Islam and to forge a synthesis of Islam's primary values and mystic folk poetry. Yunus Emre, the first great Turkish humanist, stood squarely against Muslim dogmatists in expressing the primary importance of human existence. He spoke out for human dignity and put forth an image of man not as an outcast, but as an extension of God's reality and love:

> We love the created
> For the Creator's sake.

He went in search of God's essence and, after sustained struggle and anguish, made his ultimate discovery:

> The Providence that casts this spell
> And speaks so many tongues to tell,
> Transcends the earth, heaven and hell,
> But is contained in this heart's cast.

> The yearning tormented my mind:
> I searched the heavens and the ground;
> I looked and looked, but failed to find.
> I found Him inside man at last.

Suffused throughout Yunus Emre's verses is the concept of love as the supreme attribute of man and God:

> When love arrives, all needs and flaws are gone.

He found in love a spiritual force that transcends the narrow confines into which human beings are forced:

> The man who feels the marvels of true love
> Abandons his religion and nation.

Naturalistic and ecumenical visions form an integral part of Yunus Emre's theology:

> With the mountains and rocks
> I call you out, my God;
> With the birds as day breaks
> I call you out, my God.

> With Jesus in the sky,
> Moses on Mount Sinai,
> Raising my scepter high,
> I call you out, my God.

His poems frequently refer to his full acceptance of the "four holy books" rather than to a strict adherence to the Koran—the other three books being the Old Testament, the New Testament, and the Talmud.

Many of Yunus Emre's fundamental concepts are steeped in the Sufi tradition, particularly as set forth by Rumi, who utilized the legacy of Persia in cultural and linguistic terms. Like the medieval authors and thinkers in Europe who set aside their national languages in favor of Latin, Rumi chose Persian as his vehicle of expression. But Yunus Emre, like Dante, preferred the vernacular of his own people. Because he spoke their language and gave them the sense and the succor of divine love in such lines as "Whoever has one drop of love / Possesses God's existence," he became a legendary figure and a folk saint. In his lifetime, he traveled far and wide as a "dervish," not "colonizing" like many of his fellow dervishes, but letting his poetry serve the function of *propaganda fide*. For more than seven centuries, his verses have been memorized, recited, and celebrated in the heartland of Anatolia. His fame has become so widespread that about a dozen towns claim to have his burial place.

Yunus Emre had a penchant for indigenous forms, used simple syllabic meters, and expressed his sentiments and the wisdom of his faith in the common man's language. Among his stylistic virtues are distilled statements, plain images and metaphors, and the avoidance of prolixity. He explicitly cautioned against loquaciousness and bloated language:

Too many words are fit for a beast of burden.

Yunus Emre practiced *aemulatio,* free use of living tradition, whereas others often produced *imitatio,* servile copies of earlier verses. He was able to use the forms (in particular the *gazel*), the prosody (the quantitative metric system called *aruz*), and the vocabulary of Arabic and Persian poetry. But most of his superior poems utilize the best resources of Turkish poetics, including the syllabic meters.

Yunus Emre's permanence and power emanate not merely from his language, but from his themes of timeless significance, from his universal concepts and concerns. He is very much a poet of today not only in Turkey, but around the world. We live in an age that articulates the dramatic contrast of love and hostility. War is renounced as the immediate evil and the ultimate crime against humanity. Love is recognized as the celebration of life. A mighty slogan of the 1960s and 1970s was "Make love, not war." This forceful statement is an echo from seven centuries ago, wherein we once again hear Yunus Emre, who expressed the same idea in a rhymed couplet:

> I am not here on earth for strife,
> Love is the mission of my life.

In his own age and down to the present, Yunus Emre has provided spiritual guidance and aesthetic enjoyment. His poetry is replete with universal verities and values and expresses the ecstasy of communion with nature and union with God. In his thought, the theme of union with God frequently appears as an incipient utopia. His humanism includes, in Hegel's words, the "urging of the spirit outward—that desire on the part of man to become acquainted with his world." Yunus Emre goes beyond this urge and aesthetically revels in the world's beauty. He expresses the typical humanistic joy of life:

> This world is a young bride dressed in bright red and green;
> Look on and on, you can't have enough of that bride.

Yunus Emre spurned book learning if it did not have humanistic relevance because he believed in man's godliness:

> If you don't identify Man as God,
> All your learning is of no use at all.

In this sense, he was akin to Petrarch, also a fourteenth-century poet, and to Erasmus, who, as a part of classical or Renaissance humanism a century later, shunned the dogmatism imposed on man by scholasticism and tried to instill in the average man a rejuvenated sense of the importance of his life on earth. Similar to Dante's work, Yunus Emre's poetry symbolizes the ethical patterns of mortal life while depicting the higher values of immortal being. Yunus Emre also offers to the common man "the optimism of mysticism"—the conviction that human beings, sharing godly attributes, are capable of transcending themselves:

> The image of the Godhead is a mirror;
> The man who looks sees his own face in there.

The central doctrine of Sufism is *vahdet-i vücut,* the unity of existence. Yunus Emre explicitly states this fundamental tenet:

The universe is the oneness of Deity,
The true man is he who knows this unity.

You had better seek Him in yourself,
You and He aren't apart—you're one.

"God's revelation in man" and "the human being as a true reflection of God's beautiful images" are recurrent themes in Yunus Emre's poems:

He is God Himself—human are His images.
See for yourself: God is man, that is what He is.

In an age when hostilities, rifts, and destruction were rampant, Yunus Emre was able to give expression to an all-embracing love of humanity and to concepts of universal brotherhood that transcended all schisms and sects:

For those who truly love God and His ways
All the people of the world are brothers and sisters.

Humanism upholds the ideal of the total community of mankind. Yunus Emre's humanist credo is also based on international understanding that transcends ethnic, political, and sectarian divisions:

The man who doesn't see the nations of the world as one
Is a rebel even if the pious claim he's holy.

In a similar vein, Yunus declares his belief in virtue and unitarianism:

Mystic is what they call me,
Hate is my only enemy;
I harbor a grudge against none.
To me the whole wide world is one.

Yunus Emre's view of mysticism is closely allied with the concept that all human beings are born of God's love and that they are therefore equal and worthy of peace on earth. He decried religious intolerance and dwelt on the "unity of humanity":

We regard no one's religion as contrary to ours,
True love is born when all faiths are united as a whole.

In Yunus Emre's view, service to society is the ultimate moral ideal, and the individual can find his own highest good in working for the benefit of all. His exhortations call for decent treatment of deprived people—"To look askance at the lowly is the wrong way"—and for social interdependence and charity:

> Toil, earn, eat, and give others your wages.

— — —

> Hand out to others what you earn,
> Do the poor people a good turn.

He spoke out courageously against the oppression of underprivileged people by rulers, landowners, wealthy men, officials, and religious leaders:

> Kindness of the lords ran its course,
> Now each one goes straddling a horse,
> They eat the flesh of the paupers,
> All they drink is the poor men's blood.

This humble mystic struck hard at the heartlessness of men in positions of power:

> The lords are wild with wealth and might,
> They ignore the poor people's plight;
> Immersed in selfhood which is blight,
> Their hearts are shorn of charity.

Yunus Emre also denigrated the pharisees' orthodox views and strict teachings:

> The preachers who usurp the Prophet's place
> Inflict distress and pain on the populace.

He had no use for the trappings of organized religion:

> True faith is in the head, not in the headgear.

— — —

> A single visit into the heart is
> Better than a hundred pilgrimages.

Claiming that the true believer "has no hope of Paradise nor fear of Hell," the mystic poet is capable of taking even God himself to task:

> You set a scale to weigh deeds, for your aim
> Is to hurl me into Hell's crackling flame.

You can see everything, you know me—fine;
Then, why must you weigh all these deeds of mine?

In poem after poem, he reminds the fanatics that love is supreme and that stringent rules are futile:

Yunus Emre says to you, pharisee,
Make the holy pilgrimage if need be
A thousand times—but if you ask me,
The visit to a heart is best of all.

He warns that worship is not enough; all the ablutions and obeisances will not wash away the sin of maltreatment, offense, or exploitation committed against a good person:

If you break a true believer's heart once,
It's no prayer to God—this obeisance.

Like Mansur al-Hallaj (d. 922), one of the greatest Islamic Sufis of all time, who was put to death for proclaiming, "Anal Haq" (I am God), Yunus Emre announced that he had achieved divinity:

Since the start of time I have been Mansur.
I have become God Almighty, brother.

He made a poetic plea for peace and the brotherhood of mankind—a plea for humanism that is still supremely relevant in today's world convulsing with conflict and war:

Come, let us all be friends for once,
Let us make life easy on us,
Let us be lovers and loved ones,
The earth shall be left to no one.

This medieval humanist achieved new international stature when in November 1989 the UNESCO General Conference unanimously passed a resolution declaring 1991, the 750th anniversary of the poet's birth, "The International Yunus Emre Year" in recognition of his enduring ideals of universalism, ecumenical spirit, humanitarian values, and human dignity raised to the level of divinity. That year included an extensive program of Yunus Emre activities—translations into numerous major and minor languages, symposia and seminars, telecasts and radio broadcasts, lecture series, poetry readings, and exhibitions in Turkey and in numerous other countries on all continents.

Yunus Emre's humanistic and aesthetic values, which were kept alive in Anatolia's oral tradition, have had a powerful impact on Turkish culture since the early part of the twentieth century and will likely remain influential in the future.

Ottoman Glories

THE OTTOMAN STATE had a life span of more than six centuries, from 1299 to 1922. A single dynasty reigned in unbroken continuity. Islam was not only the religious faith, but also the political ideology of the basically theocratic Ottoman state. The empire was multiracial, multinational, multireligious, multilingual. In ruling over these disparate elements, the Ottoman establishment achieved remarkable success in administrative, military, and fiscal organization.

Ottoman literature, which stressed poetry as the superior art, utilized the forms and aesthetic values of Islamic Arabo-Persian literature. The educated elite, led by the sultans (many of whom were accomplished poets themselves), produced a huge body of verse whose hallmarks included refined diction, abstruse vocabulary, euphony, romantic agony, dedication to formalism and tradition, and the Sufi brand of mysticism. Although prose was not held in high esteem by the Ottoman literary establishment, it nevertheless accounts for some excellent achievements, in particular the travelogues of the seventeenth-century cultural commentator Evliya Çelebi. The Ottoman Empire also nurtured a rich theatrical tradition, which consisted of *Karagöz* (shadow plays), *Meddah* (storyteller and impersonator), and *Orta oyunu* (a type of *commedia dell'arte*).

Three main literary traditions evolved: (1) *Tekke* (sect, denomination) literature; (2) oral folk literature; and (3) *Divan* (elite) literature. Oral folk literature and *Divan* literature hardly ever influenced each other; in fact, they remained oblivious of one another. *Tekke* literature, however, had an easy intercourse with both, utilizing their forms, prosody, vocabulary, and stylistic devices in a pragmatic fashion.

Religious *(Tekke)* poetry flourished among the mystics, the Muslim clergy, and the adherents of various doctrines and denominations. It served as the main repository of theological sectarianism and was in itself a poetry of dissent and discord. It embodied the schism between the Sunni and Shiite segments of the Muslim-Turkish population and embraced a spate of unorthodox doctrines *(tarikat),* from *tasavvuf,* libertarian mysticism, to anarchical Bektashiism and the Hurufi, Yesevi, Mevlevi, Bayrami, Alevi, Kadiri, Halveti, and Melami sects that were often hotbeds of political opposition within the theocratic system and contributed to unrest and strife in Anatolia.

Members of the *tekke*s (sect lodges, theological centers) were particularly prolific in the domain of religious verse. In the late thirteenth and early fourteenth centuries, Sultan Veled (son of Mevlana Celaleddin Rumi), Âşık Pasha (also a fervent advocate of developing the literary resources of Turkish), and Gülşehrî and Şeyyad Hamza (both early masters of Islamic poetry) set the inspirational tone that would remain the hallmark of this voluminous literature.

The fourteenth century produced a remarkable collection of religious epics, tales, and stories in verse marked by didacticism rather than by lyric artistry. These poems, composed principally for uneducated listeners, served to spread the Islamic faith.

The magnum opus of religious literature emerged in 1409: the *Mevlid-i Şerif* by Süleyman Çelebi (d. 1422), an adulation of the Prophet Muhammad chanted as a requiem among Muslim Turks. The tradition that yielded this masterpiece about the Prophet's life and the magnificence of Islam also produced many other verse narratives about the Prophet and Islam.

A great poet to lose his life because of passionate mystic verse, a form that incensed the traditionalists, was Nesimi (d. early fifteenth century). Two folk poets, Kaygusuz Abdal (fifteenth century) and Pir Sultan Abdal (sixteenth century), whose poetry represented the Alevi-Bektaşi movement (long considered heretical) and expressed a strong challenge to the orthodoxy of Islam, fired the imagination of many Anatolian communities. Even God was not spared from badinage. Kaygusuz Abdal wrote several poems that have barbs against God:

> You produced rebel slaves and cast them aside,
> You just left them there and made your exit, my God.

You built a hair-thin bridge for your slaves to walk on,
Let's see if you're brave enough to cross it, my God.

Pir Sultan Abdal challenged imperial power and local authorities in abrasive terms:

In Istanbul he must come down:
The sovereign with his empire's crown.

Legend has it that Pir Sultan Abdal became the leader of a popular uprising and urged kindred spirits to join the rebellion:

Come, soul brothers, let's band together,
Brandish our swords against the godless,
And restore the poor people's rights.

He even lambasted a judge:

You talk of faith which you don't heed,
You shun God's truth, command and creed,
A judge will always feed his own greed,
Could Satan be worse than this devil?

He defied his persecutor Hızır Pasha, who was to have him captured and hanged:

Come on, man! There, Hızır Pasha!
Your wheel is bound to break in two;
You put your faith in your sultan:
Someday, though, he will tumble too.

The following lines, attributed to Dadaloğlu (d. ca. 1868) were meant, in Pir Sultan Abdal's tradition, to fire the blood of the masses:

The state has issued an edict against us
The edict is the sultan's but the mountains are ours.

Oral folk literature, created by the collective poetic and narrative faculty of the common people of Anatolia, has been kept alive through the centuries by *ozan*s (minstrels), *saz* poets (poet-musicians), and *âşık*s (troubadours). It uses Turkic verse forms—that is, *türkü, koşma, mani, destan, semai,* and *varsağı.* Unsophisticated and based on folk wisdom, it developed a serene realism, an earthy humor, and a mellifluous lyric quality.

Köroğlu

This folk poet, who probably lived in the sixteenth century, became a legendary hero because of his rebellion against oppression and exploitation in the rural areas. Succeeding generations have celebrated him as a symbol of courage in deed and in words.

In one poem, Köroğlu challenged the Bey (Lord) of Bolu:

> Here I send my greetings to the Bey of Bolu!
> He should come up these hills and get his comeuppance
> As the rustling of arrows keeps echoing through
> And the clanking of shields resounds off the mountains.

In the same poem, Köroğlu tells the story of meeting the bey's forces:

> Then we were faced with legions of the enemy
> And on our brows appeared dark words of destiny.
> Rifles were invented—that ruined bravery:
> Now the curved sword has to stay in its sheath and rust.

But Köroğlu and his braves never lost their indomitable spirit:

> Even so, Köroğlu's fame as a hero will glow!
> Enemies will flee as I deal blow after blow,
> Covered with all that froth from my Gray Horse's mouth
> And with my trousers steeped in the blood of the foe!

When people in nearby villages heard that their hero's forces were vastly outnumbered, they rushed to give Köroğlu their support. Most of them did not even have bows and arrows, let alone rifles: they brought their pickaxes and shovels. The bey was frightened by this massive turnout of support, these multitudes ready to give their lives for the rebel cause, and he ordered his army to retreat. Köroğlu rejoiced:

> The hero holds fast, cowards flee,
> The battlefield rumbles and roars.
> Supreme king's court opens its doors:
> The palace shakes, rumbles and roars.

The proud hero will never yield.
His arrows pound the battlefield;
When his mace strikes hard at the shield
That huge shield shakes, rumbles and roars.

Arrows are shot from his fortress:
May God save you from that distress!
Hearing Köroğlu's battle cries,
Every place shakes, rumbles and roars.

Popular culture in the Ottoman state, keeping alive the Turkic rather than the Islamic patterns of thought and values, also constituted a sub-rosa system of deviation from the norms of the educated classes. Folk poetry came to typify and embody the gulf between the urban elite and the common people of the rural areas. It retained the Turks' pre-Islamic and nomadic values and regenerated them in archetypal form. Written (or composed) by ill-educated and often illiterate minstrels and troubadours, it had little susceptibility to or proclivity for the characteristics of *Divan* poetry, which boasted of erudition. The folk poet probably had scant sense of the Arabo-Persian flavor of Ottoman culture; his concern was local and autochthonous, and for purposes of direct communication he used a simple vernacular immediately intelligible to his uneducated audiences. So the substratum of indigenous culture resisted the temptation to borrow from the elite poets, who in turn were imitating their Persian and (occasionally) Arabic counterparts. In this sense, one could conceivably regard the corpus of folk poetry as a massive resistance to or a constant subversion of the values adopted by the Ottoman ruling class. It also gave voice at times to the spirit of rebellion against central authority and local feudal lords.

Anatolian minstrelsy produced such major figures as Köroğlu, the stentorian heroic poet of the sixteenth century; Karacaoğlan (seventeenth century), who wrote lilting lyrics of love and pastoral beauty; Âşık Ömer and Gevherî in the eighteenth century; and Dadaloğlu, Dertli, Bayburtlu Zihni, Erzurumlu Emrah, and Seyrani in the nineteenth century.

With its tender flakes, snow flutters about,
Keeps falling, calling out "Elif . . . Elif . . ."
This frenzied heart of mine wanders about
Like minstrels, calling out "Elif . . . Elif . . ."

Elif's robe is embroidered all over;
Her eyes—like a baby goshawk's—glower.
She smells lovely like a highland flower,
With those scents calling out "Elif . . . Elif . . ."

When she frowns, her glance is a dart that goes
Into my heart: I fall into death's throes.
In her white hand she holds a pen—she knows
What she writes, calling out "Elif . . . Elif . . ."

Right in front of her home a trellis stands;
There's Elif, holding glasses in her hands.
It's as if a duck whose head has green strands
Gently floats, calling out "Elif . . . Elif . . ."

I am the Minstrel: your slave for my part.
There's no love for other belles in my heart.
Unbuttoning the shirt, I tear apart
The collar, calling out "Elif . . . Elif . . ."

Karacaoğlan, seventeenth century

The moods of folk poetry range from tender love to angry protest. For instance, the closing lines of an old anonymous *mani* (quatrain) inquires:

There's the trace of a gaze on your face
Who has looked at you, my darling?

And in the nineteenth century, Serdari bemoaned:

The tax collector rips through the villages
His whip in hand, he tramples on the poor.

Folk literature produced a large corpus of stories, tales, allegories, fables, and riddles. The common people's dramatic imagination nurtured the *Karagöz* shadow plays. It is significant that in these plays the two principal characters, Karagöz and Hacivat, respectively represent a folksy, good-hearted simpleton and a foxy, foolish blabbermouth who tries to simulate urbane speech.

In Ottoman culture, no tragedy evolved, and comedy was confined to *Karagöz* and *commedia dell'arte (Orta oyunu)*. Tragedy places the human predicament in an identifiable setting and usually depicts personal or social rifts by dint of the vicissitudes of heroes, and comedy pokes fun at society in explicit terms. Ottoman society, in particular the establishment, conceivably had little sympathy for such representations by live actors. Or perhaps poetry was so pervasive and satisfying that authors did not consider it necessary or useful to experiment with other genres. In the vacuum, satire flourished. It performed the function of exposing folly, challenging prevailing values, unmasking hypocrisy, and denouncing injustice. In more recent times, the focal targets of satire have been morals and manners, cant, political norms, and politicians themselves.

The Ottoman elite was passionately devoted to poetry. Perhaps the crowning achievement of Ottoman culture was poetry, which also served as the propaedeutic to all other literary arts and as an element of visual and plastic arts such as calligraphy, architecture, and miniature painting as well as of the decorative arts. *Divan* poetry, as the Turkish elite poetry that was influenced by Arabic and Persian literature is often called, found favor at the court and at the coffeehouse, satisfying the aesthetic needs of both the elite and the man in the street. Significantly, two-thirds of the sultans were poets—some, in particular Mehmed "the Conqueror" (1432–81) and Süleyman the Magnificent (1494–1566), were first rate.

"Prose," as E. J. W. Gibb observed, "was as a rule reserved for practical and utilitarian purposes."[1] Poets and intellectuals spurned prose as being too easy. Nef'î, the great classical lyricist and satirist of the seventeenth century, boasted:

.

---

1. E. J. W. Gibb, *A History of Ottoman Poetry,* 6 vols. (London: Luzac, 1900–1909; reprint, Cambridge, U.K.: Trustees of the "E. J. W. Gibb Memorial," 1963–84), 1:iii.

I would not deign to write prose, but if I did
Heavenly angels would chant it time and again.

Verse often preempted the functions of prose. As a consequence, in addition to the massive output of lyric and mystic poetry, a great many didactic, theological, narrative, historical, and scholarly works were also written in verse.

These works included chronicles of war and conquest, albums of festivities and weddings, books of counsel, and other types of writing. In the nineteenth century, versifiers even came up with a chemistry textbook in poetic form and Turkish–French, Turkish–Armenian, and Turkish–Greek dictionaries in meter and rhyme.

Notwithstanding the classical poets' pejorative view of prose, a fair retrospective assessment today leads one to numerous praiseworthy prose works produced by the Ottomans: religious commentaries; narratives; epics of the fourteenth and fifteenth centuries; the histories of Âşıkpaşazade (d. 1502), Neşrî (d. second decade of the sixteenth century),[2] Lütfi Pasha (d. 1563), Âli (d. 1600), Peçevî (d. 1649?), Naima (d. 1716),[3] and Silâhtar Mehmed (d. 1724); the theological treatises of Sinan Pasha (d. 1486); the tract on ethics by Kınalızade Ali (d. 1572); the philosophical narratives of Veysî (d. 1628); and the commentaries on reforms by İbrahim Müteferrika (d. 1745), who also introduced the printing press to the Ottoman Empire, and by Koca Sekbanbaşı (d. 1804). Among the chief works of Ottoman prose are the monumental travelogues by Evliya Çelebi (d. 1682),[4] which are fascinating accounts of geography, social and economic arrangements,

2. V. L. Menage, *Neshri's History of the Ottomans* (London: Oxford Univ. Press, 1964).

3. Lewis V. Thomas, *A Study of Naima,* edited by Norman Itzkowitz (New York: New York Univ. Press, 1972); and *Annals of the Turkish Empire from 1591 to 1659 of the Christian Era,* translated by C. Fraser (London: Oriental Translation Fund, 1832).

4. Evliya Çelebi, *Narrative of Travels in Europe, Asia and Africa in the Seventeenth Century,* 2 vols., translated by Joseph von Hammer (London: Oriental Translation Fund, 1834–50). A new edition has been published in ten volumes: *Evliya Çelebi Seyahatnâmesi: Topkapı Sarayı Bağdat 304 Yazmasının Transkripsiyonu-Dizini,* vols. 1 and 7–10 edited by Yücel Dağlı, Seyit Ali Kahraman, and Robert Dankoff; vol. 2 edited by Zekeriya Kurşun, Seyit Ali Kahraman, and Yucel Dağlı; vols. 3, 4, and 6 edited by Seyit Ali Kahraman and Yücel Dağlı; vol. 5 edited by Yücel Dağlı, Seyit Ali Karaman, and İbrahim Sezgin (Istanbul: Yapı Kredi, 1999–2007).

and culture and daily life; the political and cultural commentaries by Kâtip Çelebi (d. 1658);[5] the famous essay *(Risale)* about sociopolitical reforms by Koçi Bey (seventeenth century); the ambassadorial journals of Yirmisekiz Mehmed Çelebi (d. 1732); and the semisurrealistic imaginative stories by Aziz Efendi (d. 1798).

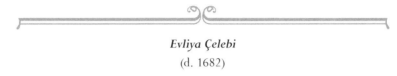

Evliya Çelebi
(d. 1682)

Evliya Çelebi never ceases to amaze. His ten-volume Seyahatname, *in unfurling the panorama of the Ottoman Empire in the seventeenth century, defies genres. It is geography and history, sociology and literature, databank and euhemerism. Its bland title, which simply signifies "Book of Travels," is an expression of humility from the author-narrator, who frequently refers to himself as humble, lowly, and poor. In its sweep and thrust,* Seyahatname *invites comparison with the writings of Strabo, Procopius, Marco Polo, and Ibn Battuta. Passages from it read like Carlyle and Rabelais, Pepys and Pater. In Evliya Çelebi's sprawling saga of the Ottoman world lies an immensely rich source of precise information as well as hearsay and flights of imagination for scholars in the Ottoman field to draw on and to savor. One must savor it, to be sure, because this travelogue is also an engrossing literary work that comes close to ranking as the Ottoman prose masterpiece.*

Ottoman literature produced no literary criticism except for biographies, bibliographies, and superficial commentaries. Referred to as *tezkire'tüş-şuara,* these works are little more than a "Who's Who in Ottoman Poetry."[6] Among the best specimens are those produced in the sixteenth century by Sehî, Lâtifî, Âşık Çelebi, and Kınalızade Hasan. The

5. Katip Çelebi, *The Balance of Truth,* translated by Geoffrey Lewis (London: Allen and Unwin, 1957).

6. Joseph von Hammer-Purgstall's *Geschichte der osmanischen Dichtkunst,* 4 vols. (Pest: C. A. Hartleben, 1836–38), is a massive compilation of the biographies of about 2,200 Turkish poets. This reference book is a German version of the typical *tezkire.*

glaring fact is that Ottoman literature from its beginnings until the second half of the nineteenth century functioned in a critical vacuum, aside from extravagant sycophantic praises or scathing satire that one finds—and immediately dismisses as worthless—in some poets' work.

Divan poetry was composed by and for an intellectual elite affiliated mostly with the court. Most of the prominent poets received a theological education at a *medrese* (Muslim academy), where instruction was given in Arabic and Persian, both considered a sine qua non for a man of letters. The Ottoman poets as a rule viewed it as the epitome of literary achievement to publish a collection of poems in one of these two languages—or preferably in both. Fuzuli (d. 1556), ranked among the two or three greatest classical poets, wrote three *divan*s (collections of poems)—in Turkish, Arabic, and Persian.

From beginning to end, classical poetry remained under the pervasive influence of Persian and Arabic poetry: it imitated and tried to emulate the verse forms, rhyme-and-rhythm patterns, meters, mythology, and even Weltanschauung of the Persian and Arabic masters. It also adopted a substantial portion of their vocabulary.

Aruz (Arabic: *arud*), a quantitative prosody devised by the Arabs and perfected by the Persians, dominated *Divan* poetry. This metric form is based on the arrangement of syllables according to vowel length and consonantal ending. Each short vowel at the end of a syllable accounts for a short sound (·). A syllable ending in a consonant or a long vowel is taken as a long sound (–). The meter of one famous line would thus be:

Â-şık ol-dur kim kı-lar câ-nın fe-dâ câ-nâ-nı-na
– · – – / – · – – / – · – – / – · –

In this complaint by Fuzuli, that "The lover is he who sacrifices his life to his loved one," the meter as it stands is one of the most frequently used. The name of the meter is *Fâilâtün / fâilâtün / fâilâtün / fâilün,* which reproduces the sound pattern. The final *k* of *âşık* is linked with the word *oldur,* and the final syllable of the line, as in the case of all meters, is automatically accepted as long even though it ends in a short vowel. The poet could choose from about a hundred different meters.

This prosodic structure was essentially ill suited to Turkish phonology. *Aruz* meters have a preponderance of long syllables, whereas Turkish makes frequent use of short vowels. Three successive short syllables, for instance, can be used only at the end of just a few meters, and no meter can accommodate four successive short syllables. (The name "A-na-do-lu," meaning Anatolia, to cite one blatant example, cannot fit any *aruz* meter.) This incongruity caused two anomalous situations: it forced poets to distort the pronunciation of hundreds of Turkish words in order to fit them into the molds of the meters and to borrow a huge number of Persian and Arabic words with long vowels. The prosody afforded definite rhythms and predetermined euphonic structures, which, as pleasing to the ear as they certainly are, can become repetitive and tedious to the point where the substance is virtually subjugated to the meter.

Divan poetry also used the major verse forms of Persian and Arabic literatures: *gazel,* the lyric ode, with a minimum of five and a maximum of fifteen couplets (*aa / ba / ca / da / ea*); *kaside* (often used for the panegyric, with the same rhyme pattern as the *gazel,* but running as long as thirty-three to ninety-nine couplets); *mesnevi* (self-rhyming couplets by the hundreds or thousands used for narratives or didactic works); *rubai* (the quatrain *a / a / b / a* expressing a distilled idea); *tuyuğ* (a quatrain utilizing a specific *aruz* meter); *şarkı* (originally called *murabba,* often used for lyrics of love and levity); and *musammat* (extended versions of many of the other basic verse forms).

Form reigned supreme over *Divan* poetry. Content, most *Divan* poets felt, should be the self-generating substance whose concepts and values were not to be questioned, let alone renovated. As in the case of the performance of classical music in the West, craftsmanship was creative artistry, virtuosity was virtue.

Despite the tyranny of form, which even forced on the poet the requirement that each poetic statement be contained within the couplet or distich and that a static metaphorical system be regenerated with such sets of conceptual congruity as the *gül*, the rose representing the beautiful sweetheart, and the *bülbül,* the distraught nightingale symbolizing the eloquent poet in love, prominent *Divan* poets attained a profound spirituality, a trenchant sensitivity, an overflowing eroticism. The themes recurring in the work of the masters range from self-glorification to self-abnegation, from agony to ebullient joy, from fanatic abstinence to uninhibited hedonism. Islamic mysticism, as the soul's passionate yearning to merge with God, constitutes the superstructure of much *Divan* poetry.[7]

Among the early masters of the *Divan* tradition are Ahmedî (d. 1413), Ahmed Pasha (d. 1497), Ahmed-i Dâi (fourteenth–fifteenth century), and Necatî (d. 1509). In the early fifteenth century, Şeyhî, a physician-poet, wrote one of the most remarkable satires of socioeconomic inequity, a verse allegory called "Harname" (The Donkey Story), in which he contrasted a starving donkey with well-fed oxen:

> Once there was a feeble donkey, pining away,
> Bent under the weight of his load, he used to bray.
>
> Carrying wood here and water there was his plight.
> He felt miserable, and languished day and night.
>
> So heavy were the burdens he was forced to bear
> That the sore spots on his skin left him without hair.
>
> His flesh and skin, too, nearly fell off his body;
> Under his loads, from top to toe, he was bloody.
>
> Whoever saw his appearance remarked, in fact,
> "Surprising that this bag of bones can walk intact!"
>
> His lips dangled, and his jaws had begun to droop;
> He got tired if a fly rested on his croup.
>
> Goose pimples covered his body whenever he saw,
> With those starving eyes, just a handful of straw.
>
> On his ears there was an assembly of crows;
> Over the slime of his eyes flies marched in rows.
>
> Whenever the saddle was taken off his rumps,
> What remained looked altogether like a dog's dumps.

7. Talat S. Halman, "Turkish Poetry," in *The New Princeton Encyclopaedia of Poetry and Poetics*, edited by Alex Preminger and T. V. F. Brogan (Princeton, N.J.: Princeton Univ. Press, 1993), 1311–314.

One day, his master decided to show pity,
And for once he treated the beast with charity:

He took the saddle off, let him loose on the grass;
As he walked on, while grazing, suddenly the ass

Saw some robust oxen pacing the pastureland:
Their eyes were fiery and their buttocks grand.

With all the grass they gobbled up, they were so stout
That if one hair were plucked, all that fat would seep out.

Jauntily they walked, carefree, their hearts filled with zest;
Summer sheds, winter barns, and nice places to rest.

No halter's pain for them nor the saddle's anguish,
No heavy loads causing them to wail or languish.

Struck with wonder and full of envy, he stood there,
Brooding over his own plight which was beyond compare:

We were meant to be the equals of these creatures,
We have the same hands and feet, same forms and features.

Why then is the head of each ox graced by a crown
And why must poverty and dire need weigh us down?

This depiction of oxen graced by crowns was certainly courageous as satire because the target in the allegory could well have been the sultan and his entourage.

Fuzuli, the great figure of Ottoman literature in the sixteenth century, emerged at the peak of the Ottoman Empire's grandeur. He is the author of the *mesnevi* entitled *Leylâ vü Mecnun* (*Leylā and Mejnūn*[8]), a long narrative poem close to four thousand couplets that explores the philosophical implications of worldly and mystic love.

Perhaps no other poet exerted as much influence as Fuzuli on the elite poetry of the succeeding few centuries. Among his most memorable lines are:

---

8. Fuzuli, *Leylā and Mejnūn,* translated by Sofi Huri (London: Allen and Unwin, 1970).

I wish I had a thousand lives in this broken heart of mine
So I could sacrifice myself to you once with each one.

— — —

The state is topsy-turvy like a cypress reflected on water.

I reap no gains but trouble at your place when I come near;
My wish to die on your love's path is all that I hold dear.

I am the reed-flute when griefs assemble. Cast to the winds
What you find in my burnt-up, dried-up body except desire.

May bloody tears draw curtains on my face the day we part
So that my eyes will see just that moon-faced love when they peer.

My loneliness has grown to such extremes that not a soul
Except the whirlwind of disaster spins within my sphere.

There's nobody to burn for my sake but my heart's own fire;
My door is opened by none other than the soft zephyr.

O waves, don't ravage all my surging teardrops, for this flood
Has caused all welfare buildings save this one to disappear.

The rites of love are on; how can the poet hold his sighs:
Except for sound, what profit could be found in me to clear?

Fuzuli, sixteenth century

Hayalî (d. 1557), Yahya of Taşlıca (d. 1582), Şeyhülislâm Yahya (d. 1644), and Nailî (d. 1666) achieved well-deserved renown for virtuosity, graceful lyricism, and an elegant use of the language. Baki, the great sixteenth-century poet laureate, attained wide fame for the aesthetic perfection of his secular *gazel*s and *kaside*s:

With all our heart, we're at love's beck and call:
We don't resist the will of fate at all.

We never bow to knaves for this vile world;
In God we trust, we're only in His thrall.

We don't rely on the state's golden staff—
The grace of God grants us our wherewithal.

Although our vices shock the universe,
We want no pious acts to save our soul.

Thank God, all earthly glory must perish,
But Baki's name endures on the world's scroll.

Because *Divan* literature was inundated by Arabic and Persian vocabulary, much of it arcane and inaccessible, some poets opted for a more dominant use of words of Turkish origin. This "re-Turkification" process received impetus from literary precedents. In the first half of the sixteenth century, for instance, a movement called *türki-i basit* (Simple Turkish), led by Nazmi of Edirne (d. after 1554) and Mahremî of Tatavla (d. ca. 1536), advocated the use of colloquial Turkish, free of Arabic and Persian borrowings and of all Persian *izafet* formulations, in the classical stanzaic forms utilizing the Arabic-Persian prosody *(aruz),* and showed, on the strength of their large and impressive output, that success could be achieved along these lines, pointing to the emergence of an original body of "national literature."[9]

Ottoman elite poetry has often been criticized for being too abstract, too repetitious, and excessively divorced from society and concrete reality. Modernists in the latter part of the nineteenth century took the classical poets to task for having abandoned the mainstream of Turkish national literary tradition in favor of servile imitations of Arabic and Persian poetry. In republican Turkey, not only the advocates of folk poetry and modern European poetry, but also a prominent scholar of Ottoman literature, Abdülbaki Gölpınarlı (d. 1982), launched frontal attacks on this elite poetry.[10] Among the principal objections were stringent formalism, abstract substance and formulations, frozen metaphors and cliché images, and a masochistic and misogynistic view of love and life.

---

9. Köprülüzade Mehmed Fuad (Mehmed Fuad Köprülü), *Milli Edebiyat Cereyanının İlk Mübeşşirleri ve Divan-ı Türki-i Basit* (Istanbul: Türk Dil Kurumu, 1918).

10. Abdülbaki Gölpınarlı, *Divan Edebiyatı Beyanındadır* (Istanbul: Marmara, 1945).

Although there is a measure of truth in these critical comments, *Divan* poetry achieved impressive success as *poésie pure* with a commitment, in Platonic terms, to abstraction's being more real than reality itself. The auditory imagination operative in its aesthetics never fails to impress the sensitive ear. Although it may be steeped in evocations of *la belle dame sans merci,* the emotional dimensions that the most accomplished classical poets such as Fuzuli and Şeyh Galib (d. 1799) establish in their poems sway the romantic souls on one level and the cerebral readers on another. And despite much repetition of metaphor and stock epithets, *Divan* poets offer innumerable fresh, compelling, imaginative metaphors and images.

Baki's proverbial line, which posits the supremacy of eloquent sound in a fleeting world, still holds true:

> What endures in this dome is but a pleasant echo.

The mystic strain seems to have embodied the sense of alienation experienced by the Ottoman intellectual. A famous couplet by Neşatî (d. 1674) epitomizes this feeling:

> We have so removed our physical existence
> We are now hidden in the gleaming mirror.

The same sense of dissociation from reality in its worldly or external aspects, the anguish of exile, and the sorrow of spiritual banishment that run through Ottoman mystic poetry are not simply the stock sentiments of Islamic Sufism, but also statements of discontent about the structure and functioning of society. The tone is almost always pessimistic and often nihilistic, albeit in anticipation of ultimate happiness. A sullen craft and art, the poetry of the mystics nurtured a special branch of literature, as it were—a literature of complaint, chronic dissatisfaction, and disenchantment with the times. Fuzuli voiced this gloomy attitude in many well-known lines:

> Friends are heartless, the world ruthless, time without peace,
> Trouble abounds, no one befriends you, the foe is strong, fortune is
> weak.
>
> — — —
>
> Rifts are rampant, the community of peace is rent with fear,
> I am at a loss, for I can find no true pathfinder.

Within the theocratic framework, the poets saw and showed the sultan as sacrosanct. Ottoman panegyrics charted a progression of love—from an ordinary sweetheart to the sultan and ultimately to God. In fact, in many Ottoman poems written by the court poets as well as by the independents and mystics, a three-level interpretation of the "beloved" is possible: darling, king, and divine being.

This progression—or perhaps deliberate obfuscation—growing in concentric circles is reinforced by the attribution of absolute beauty *(cemâl-i mutlak)* and absolute perfection *(kemâl-i mutlak)* to God. The element of *celâl* (implying might, greatness, and awesome presence) also figures prominently. So the composite picture of the "loved one," of the sultan, and of God in *Divan* literature is one of inaccessibility, beauty, glory, and cruelty. In a much subtler conception than mere masochism, the *Divan* metaphor equates beauty with pain and strives to arrive at *pathei mathos*— that is, wisdom through suffering. In a sense, establishment poets seemed to present the sultan or any person in power as having the divine right— like God—to inflict pain and misery. The mystics, in their insistence on the human predicament whereby separation from God is woeful, intensified the myth—particularly when they offered the ideals of love's torture and self-sacrifice.

The metaphorical progression from the "beloved" to the sultan and farther on to God had its concomitant of complaint. Prostration became, in effect, a form of protest:

> Fuzuli is a beggar imploring your grace's favor;
> Alive he is your dog, dead he is dust at your feet.
> Make him live or die, the judgment and the power are yours,
> My vision my life my master my loved one my royal Sultan.

Because the poets frequently bemoaned their suffering at the hands of the loved one, the complaint was thereby about the sultan and about God, whose will the sultan represented on earth.

Those sultans who were themselves poets also contributed to the view of their reign as being less valuable than love, in particular the love of God. Mehmed "the Conqueror" (d. 1481) expressed this concept in a pithy line:

> I am the slave of a Sultan whose slave is the world's sultan.

Love letter in poetic form sent by Sultan Süleyman the Magnificent to his wife, Hürrem

My very own queen, my everything, my beloved, my bright moon;
My intimate companion, my one and all, sovereign of all
   beauties, my sultan.

My life, the gift I own, my be-all, my elixir of Paradise, my Eden,
My spring, my joy, my glittering day, my exquisite one who smiles
   on and on.

My sheer delight, my revelry, my feast, my torch, my sunshine,
   my sun in heaven;
My orange, my pomegranate, the flaming candle that lights up
   my pavilion.

My plant, my candy, my treasure who gives no sorrow but the
   world's purest pleasure;
Dearest, my turtledove, my all, the ruler of my heart's Egyptian
   dominion.

My Istanbul, my Karaman, and all the Anatolian lands that are
   mine;
My Bedakhshan and my Kipchak territories, my Baghdad and my
   Khorasan.

My darling with that lovely hair, brows curved like a bow, eyes
   that ravish: I am ill.
If I die, yours is the guilt. Help, I beg you, my love from a
   different religion.

I am at your door to glorify you. Singing your praises, I go on
   and on:
My heart is filled with sorrow, my eyes with tears. I am the
   Lover—this joy is mine.

   Muhibbi (Sultan Süleyman's pen name), sixteenth century

Kanuni Süleyman (better known in the West as Süleyman the Magnificent), like many other sultan-poets, including Selim I, Ahmed I, Mustafa III, and Selim III, denigrated worldly power, choosing to glorify the supremacy of love:

> What they call reigning is nothing but worldly quarrel;
> There is no greater throne on the earth than the love of God.

So it devolved on the fifteenth-century poet Ali Şîr Nevâî to indicate the focal significance of the monarchy in mystical as well as political terms:

> Away from the loved one, the heart is a country without a king,
> And that country stands as a body whose life and soul are lacking.
>
> Tell me, Muslims, what good is a body without its life and soul—
> Just black earth that nurtures no life-giving basil or rose of spring
>
> And the black earth where no life-giving basil or sweet roses grow
> Resembles the darkest of nights in which the moon has stopped gleaming.
>
> Oh, Nevâî, tortures abound, but the worst punishment is when
> Separation's pain is all and reunion's solace is nothing.

A thorough study of the ramifications of the darling–king–divine triad, which is offered here more in speculation than in substantiation, would give us a new understanding of *Divan* poetry—in particular mystic poetry—as a massive subversive literature, a strong protest about ruthless rule by the sultan who dispenses cruelty even though his subjects profess their love for him.

Seen in this light, the sultan, metaphorically depicted, is a ruthless tyrant who symbolizes cruel love, a supreme being, like God, who has no feelings for his suppliants. Mystic poetry eventually lost its nonconformist function when it veered away from its original concept of man as an extension of God and instead insisted on the bondage of the lover to God the beloved, thereby becoming almost identical with the orthodox view of "submission" and suffered a weakening of its valuation of man as possessing godly attributes. But Ottoman mystic poetry in general validates Péguy's observation: "Tout commence en mystique et finit en politique."

By and large, *Divan* poetry conformed almost subserviently to the empire. An empire can seldom afford to be empirical, and its literature runs the risk of becoming empyrean. So the conformist poets, perpetuating the same norms and values century after century, offering only variations on unchanging themes, and looking to virtuosity as the highest literary virtue, wrote celebrations of the triad of the Ottoman system: dynasty, faith, and conquest. When no special occasion was being committed to verse, these "establishment poets" turned out lyrics of private joy and agony sufficiently safe as comments on life and couched in abstractions. That is why *Divan* poetry is often characterized as having been "hermetically sealed" from life.

In my opinion, however, this "house organ" aspect of Ottoman poetry has been oversimplified and overemphasized. The empire also produced a large body of nonconformist, subversive protest poetry.

Taken in its entirety and in anagogic terms, mystic poetry may be regarded as a continuing opposition to and an undermining of the theocratic establishment—a quiet, undeclared war against central authority. Not only by refusing to serve as the amanuensis of imperial glory, but also, far more significantly, by insisting on the supremacy of love over "cardinal virtues," by passing over the sultan in favor of absolute allegiance to God, by ascribing the highest value to the afterlife and denouncing mundane involvements, and by rallying against the orthodox views and institutions of Islam, the mystics not only maintained a stand as "independent" spirits that in itself was detrimental to a literature and culture seeking to be monolithic, but that also eroded entrenched institutions and endeavored to explode some of the myths of the empire. So although the palace poets subserved, most of those poets outside of the cultural hierarchy subverted. The mystics maintained over the centuries a vision of apocalypse not only in a metaphysical but also in a political sense.

Many *Divan* poets protested against the chasm between the rich and the poor. In the sixteenth century, Yahya of Taşlıca wrote:

> The poor must survive on one slice of bread,
> The lord devours the world and isn't fed.
>
> — — —
>
> He who gives a poor man's heart sorrow,
> May his breast be pierced by God's arrow.

Janissary commander and poet Gazi Giray, at the end of the sixteenth century, sent the following report in verse to the sultan about impending defeat and disaster:

Infidels routed the lands which belong to true Muslims,
You have no fear of God, you take bribes and just sit there.

If no action is taken, this country is as good as lost,
If you don't believe what I say, ask anyone in the world.

From: *Elegy to the Cat*

I.

He's dead and gone! Alas! What shall I do? Pity, pussy!
The flames of death devoured you! A calamity, pussy!
The lion of doom tricked and mauled you: Woe is me, pussy!
Alas! What shall I do now? O, pity, pretty pussy!

III.

That cat of mine was so playful, such a wonderful guy.
He had a grand time catching the birds that fly in the sky.
He'd eat anything he got—a roll, a patty, a pie.
Alas! What shall I do now? O, pity, pretty pussy!

IV.

Sure, he caught sparrows just like that, but hens and geese as well;
Great fighter, he even turned the lion's life into hell;
Soldier of faith, he'd kill mice as though they were the infidel.
Alas! What shall I do now? O, pity, pretty pussy!

VII.

Fearless like a lion, a ferocious beast in combat . . .
You think he was old? No, he was a young and sprightly cat:
Every hair of his whiskers was a scimitar, that's that.
Alas! What shall I do now? O, pity, pretty pussy!

Me'âlî, sixteenth century

There were also animadversions against tyranny. Pir Mahmut wrote in the latter part of the fourteenth century:

The oppressed who stay awake and moan from torment
Will bring on their oppressors' dismemberment.

In the sixteenth century, Usûlî defied the sultan with the following words:

We never bow our heads to this land's crown and throne,
On our own thrones we are sultans in our own right.

Also in the sixteenth century, Ruhi of Baghdad, a vehement critic of the establishment, railed against the peddlers of status:

What good is a lofty place if it has its price,
Boo to the base fellow who sells it, boo to the buyer.

Ruhi distilled the theme of inequity into one couplet:

Hungry for the world, some people work nonstop
While some sit down and joyfully eat the world up.

Numerous poems of protest and complaint were directed against not the central government, but the local authorities and religious judges. In the fifteenth century, Andelibî denounced a judge for taking bribes:

Go empty-handed, his honor is asleep, they say;
Go with gold, they say: "Sir, please come this way."

Some poets offered critical views of Ottoman life and manners in *kaside*s (long odes) and *mesnevi*s (narrative poems). Among these poems, the detailed commentaries by Osmanzade Taib (d. 1724) on commodity shortages, black-market operations and profiteering, the plight of the poor people, and the indifference of the officials and judges are particularly noteworthy.

The nineteenth-century satirist İzzet Molla wrote many verses in which he denounced prominent public servants by name. In the following quatrain built on satiric puns, his victims are Yasinizade and Halet, names that can roughly be translated as "Prayer" and "State":

Mr. Prayer and Mr. State joined hands
To inflict all this on the populace:
One brought it into a state of coma,
The other gave his prayers for solace.

The great debate through the course of *Divan* poetry was between the mystic and the orthodox, the independent spirit and the fanatic, the nonconformist and the dogmatist, the latitudinarian and the zealot (*rind* versus *zahid*), who hurled insults at each other.

In the early fifteenth century when Nesimi was being skinned alive for heresy, the religious dignitary who had decreed his death was on hand watching the proceedings. Shaking his finger, the mufti said: "This creature's blood is filthy. If it spills on anyone, that limb must be cut off at once." Right then, a drop of blood squirted onto the mufti's finger. Someone said: "Sir, there is a drop of blood on your finger. According to your pronouncement, your finger should be chopped off." Scared, the mufti protested: "That won't be necessary because just a little bit of water will wash this off." Hearing this, Nesimi produced the following couplet *in extempore* and in flawless prosody while being skinned alive:

> With his finger cut, the pharisee will flee from God's truth,
> They strip this poor believer naked, yet he doesn't even cry.

The supreme satirist of Ottoman literature was Nef'î (d. 1635), who put down a conventional theologian with the following invective:

> The wily pharisee is bound by beads of fraud;
> The rosary he spins becomes the web of cant.

In addition to resonant panegyrics, Nef'î wrote many devastating poems lampooning hypocrisy and affectation. In a famous quatrain, he gave the following retort to Şeyhülislâm Yahya, the empire's chief religious dignitary at the time as well as a prominent poet:

> So the Mufti has branded me an infidel:
> In turn I shall call him a Muslim, let us say.
> The day will come for both of us to face judgment
> And we shall both emerge as liars that day.

Nef'î once devastated the orthodox theologian Hoca Tahir Efendi in four lines utilizing a play on the word *tahir*, which means "clean":

> Mr. Clean, they say, has called me a dog;
> This word displays his compliment indeed,

For I belong to the Maliki sect:
A dog is clean according to my creed.

Poetry was an Ottoman passion not only for men, but also for women who reveled in listening to or reading poems. Some women composed impressive poems in the formidably difficult conventional forms and meters. From the fifteenth century until the end of the empire in 1922, they produced a considerable number of polished verses, vying with the best of their male counterparts and often achieving prominence.

Zeyneb, who died in 1474, was a cultivated lady. This first major Ottoman woman poet was also a fine musician. One of her couplets is symptomatic of the male domination that in Ottoman society as well as in many others often made female poets follow the aesthetic norms established by men:

Zeyneb, renounce womanly fondness for the decorative life;
Like men, be simple of heart and tongue, shun flashy embellishment.

In the following exquisite quatrain, she expresses the pain of love. The second line refers to the story of Joseph, who was regarded as the embodiment of ideal human beauty, in the Koran's twelfth sura.

To you, O Lord, those enchanting looks are God's grace:
The story of Joseph is a verse from your lovely face.
Your beauty and love, your tortures and my endurance
Never ebb or end, but grow in eternal time and space.

Mihri Hatun (d. 1506) proclaims women's—and her own—superiority over men in the prefatory verse of her *divan* (collected poems):

Since, they say, woman has no brains or wit,
Whatever she speaks, they excuse it.

But your humble servant Mihri demurs
And states with that mature wisdom of hers:

Far better to have one woman with class
Than a thousand males all of whom are crass;

I would take one woman with acumen
Over a thousand muddleheaded men.

Mihri Hatun

(d. 1506)

This woman poet lived a free life of lovemaking and levity. Her beauty was legendary, and she had affairs with some of the celebrities of her time. For many years, she was a member of the intellectual circle around Prince Ahmed. When she was criticized for her affairs, she struck back in verse:

At one glance
I loved you
With a thousand hearts

They can hold against me
No sin except my love for you
Come to me
Don't go away

Let the zealots think
Loving is sinful
Never mind
Let me burn in the hellfire
Of that sin

One of Mihri's most accomplished poems is a gazel (lyric ode). Her mention of Alexander is a reference to her lover İskender.

I woke, opened my eyes, raised my head: There with his face bright
And exquisite like the full moon, he was standing upright.

Was it my lucky star, was I blessed with divine power?
In my field of vision, Jupiter ascended tonight.

He looked like a Muslim, but was wearing pagan garments;
From his enchanting face—I saw clearly—came streaming light.

By the time I had opened and closed my eyes, he vanished:
He was—I divined—a heavenly angel or a sprite.

Mihri shall never die: She found the elixir of life,
She saw Alexander beaming in the dark of the night.

Another remarkable woman poet was Leylâ Hanım (d. 1847). Her marriage lasted one week. Many of her own love poems were presumably addressed to women. By the standards of her day, she led a liberated life. Some of her daring verses scandalized the moralists of the period.

> Drink all you want in the rose-garden. Who cares what they say!
> Better enjoy life to the hilt. Who cares what they say!
>
> Could it be that my cruel lover sees my tears as dewdrops?
> Like a blooming rose, s/he is all smiles. Who cares what they say!
>
> I am your lover and your loyal slave, my beautiful—
> And shall remain so till Doomsday. Who cares what they say . . .
>
> I see my rival is chasing you—Come lie beside me.
> You say No? Well, then, so much for you. Who cares what they say.
>
> Leylâ, indulge in pleasure with your lovely, moon-faced friend;
> Make sure you pass all your days in joy. Who cares what they say!

After serving its function of heralding change and once established in its genre and confident in its intellectual orientation, *Divan* poetry remained recalcitrant to internal change. It was only after several centuries of sclerotic continuity that *Divan* verse introduced various formal and substantive changes. A significant innovation was undertaken by Nedim (d. 1730), the poet of the so-called Tulip Age, who lived la dolce vita and wrote of Sardanapalian pleasures. He dropped his predecessors' abstractions and hackneyed clichés in favor of depictions of physical beauty (aesthetic, human, and topographical), made an attempt to "democratize" conventional verse by increasing its appeal through greater intelligibility, and dispensed with the masochistic and misogynistic implications of the *Divan* poetry of the previous centuries, replacing them with the joys of love and living.

Şeyh Galib, the last of the great romantic mystics of the eighteenth century, also made an important renovation by getting away from the clichés and the frozen conceits and by making original metaphors a new vehicle of artistic expression in his masterwork *Hüsn ü Aşk* (*Beauty and Love*[11]), an alle-

---

11. Şeyh Galib, *Beauty and Love,* translated by Victoria Rowe Holbrook (New York: Modern Language Association of America, 2005).

gorical work of passionate mysticism. Galib, who served as a sheikh—that is, Mevlevi leader—in Istanbul, was profoundly influenced by Rumi's spirituality and poetics and emphatically acknowledged his impact. Among Şeyh Galib's masterful verses is a superb onomatopoeic invitation to whirling:

Edvar-ı çarha uy, mevlevi ol:
Seyran edersin, devran edersin.

Song

Come, let's grant joy to this heart of ours that founders in distress:
Let's go to the pleasure gardens, come, my sauntering cypress.
Look, at the quay, a six-oared boat is waiting in readiness—
Let's go to the pleasure gardens, come, my sauntering cypress.

Let's laugh and play, let's enjoy the world to the hilt while we may
Drink nectar at the fountain which was unveiled the other day,
And watch the gargoyle spatter the elixir of life away—
Let's go to the pleasure gardens, come, my sauntering cypress.

First, for a while, let's take a stroll around the pond in leisure,
And gaze in marvel at that palace of heavenly pleasure;
Now and then, let's sing songs or recite poems for good measure—
Let's go to the pleasure gardens, come, my sauntering cypress.

Get your mother's leave, say it's for holy prayers this Friday:
Out of time's tormenting clutches let you and I steal a day,
And slinking through the secret roads and alleys down to the quay,
Let's go to the pleasure gardens, come, my sauntering cypress.

Just you and I, and a singer with exquisite airs—and yet
Another: with your kind permission, Nedim, the mad poet.
Let's forget our boon companions today, my joyful coquette—
Let's go to the pleasure gardens, come, my sauntering cypress.

Nedim, eighteenth century

My darling with the rosy face—at one glance—
You turned my heart's mirror into a wine glass,
Passing on to me your joy and nonchalance . . .
Here's my heart, for you to ignore or to grace:
May the home of my heart be your drinking place.

Such a flame has the candle of the spirit
That the dome of the skies cannot contain it;
Not even Mount Sinai saw from its summit
The lightning bolts that my chest nurtures within it:
My bosom is up in flames thanks to your grace.

Over the apex, the royal falcon flies
Ignoring the hunt of the bird of paradise;
Nesting in your hair is a joy it denies.
Show mercy, O king, who rides the horse of the skies:
To which your generous hand gives sustenance.

In a new realm where my life has come upon,
Each dewdrop looms as enormous as the sun
And no barrier can block the sunbeams, none.
Where I arrive might be close at hand or gone:
There, your absence is the same as your embrace.

Şeyh Galib, eighteenth century

The couplet reproduces perfectly the rhythmic pattern of whirling. It is rife with mystic connotations. *Edvar-ı çarh* means the Mevlevi style of whirling as well as the revolving arches of the sky, the wheels of fortune, and the firmament. *Seyran* refers to a "pleasure trip" but also signifies a dream, gazing at a lovely sight, and contemplation. *Devran* refers to whirling, transcendence of time, the wheels of fortune, and blissful life. Combining these various implications, Şeyh Galib's couplet can be translated as

Join the heavenly circles, become a Mevlevi:
You can whirl and dream and gaze and turn and revel.

Although the classical tradition continued until the early part of the twentieth century, after Şeyh Galib it produced few figures or works of significance.

Timeless Tales

FOLKTALES, SECOND ONLY TO POETRY, have been alive as a constant genre in Turkish literature. A great many traditional Turkish tales were and still are introduced with the following *tekerleme* (a formulaic jingle with numerous variants):

> A long, long time ago,
> when the sieve was inside the straw,
> when the donkey was the town crier
> and the camel was the barber . . .
> Once there was; once there wasn't.
> God's creatures were as plentiful as grains
>   and talking too much was a sin . . .

In this lilting overture, one finds the spirit and some of the essential features of the Turkish folktale: the vivid imagination, irreconcilable paradoxes, rhythmic structure (with built-in syllabic meters and internal rhymes), a comic sense bordering on the absurd, a sense of the mutability of the world, the aesthetic urge to avoid loquaciousness, the continuing presence of the past, and the narrative's predilection to maintain freedom from time and place.

In Anatolia's culture, oral literature has played a vibrant role since the earliest times. Aesop came from Phrygia, whose capital, Gordion, stood on a site not far from Ankara, the capital of modern Turkey. Homer was probably born and reared near present-day Izmir and wandered up and down the Aegean coast amassing the tales and legends that came to be enshrined in his *Iliad* and *Odyssey*.

Several millennia of the narrative arts have bequeathed to Asia Minor a dazzling treasury—creation myths, Babylonian stories, *The Epic of Gilgamesh,*

Hittite tales, biblical lore, Greek and Roman myths, Armenian and Byzantine anecdotes. The peninsula's mythical and historical ages nurtured dramatic accounts of deities, kings, heroes, and lovers. Pagan cults, ancient faiths, the Greek pantheon, Judaism, Roman religions, Christianity, Islam, mystical sects, and diverse spiritual movements left behind an inexhaustible body of legends and moralistic stories that survived throughout the centuries in their original forms or in many modified versions. Anatolia's narrative art is a testament to the Turkish passion for stories about heroism, love, and honor.

As the Turks embraced Islam and its civilization and founded the Selçuk state (mid–eleventh century) and then the Ottoman state (in the closing years of the thirteenth century), they developed a passion for the rich written and oral literature of the Arabs and Persians. Having brought along their own indigenous narratives in their horizontal move from Central Asia to Asia Minor, they now acquired the vertical heritage of the earlier millennia of Anatolian cultures, cults, and epic imagination as well as the Islamic narrative tradition in its Arabo-Persian context. The resulting synthesis was to yield a vast reservoir of stories. It would also give impetus to the creation of countless new tales down through the ages, for all ages.

The synthesis was significantly enriched by the lore of Islamic mysticism. Romantic and didactic *mesnevi*s (long narratives composed in rhymed couplets) compelled the elite poets' attention. Perhaps the most profoundly influential masterpiece of the genre was the *Mesnevi* written in Persian by the prominent thirteenth-century Sufi thinker Mevlana Celaleddin Rumi (1207–73). Referred to as the "Koran of Mysticism" and the "Inner Truth of the Koran," this massive work of close to twenty-six thousand couplets comprises a wealth of mystico-moralistic tales, fables, and stories of wisdom.

Ottoman elite poets produced—often with the inspiration or story lines they took from *The Thousand and One Nights, Kalila wa Dimna,* Firdawsi's *Shahnamah,* Attar's *Mantiq at-Tayr,* Nizami's *Khamsa* (Five Narratives), and many others—impressive *mesnevi*s, including *Leyla vü Mecnun* (*Leylā and Mejnūn*[1]) by Fuzuli (d. 1556) and *Hüsn ü Aşk (Beauty*

---

1. Fuzuli, *Leylā and Mejnūn,* translated by Sofi Huri (London: Allen and Unwin, 1970).

and Love) by Şeyh Galib (d. 1799), both allegories of mystical love; *Hikâyat-i Deli Birader* (Mad Brother's Anecdotes), a garland of humorous and salacious stories by Mehmed Gazali (d. 1535); and *Şevkengiz,* a funny debate between a ladies' man and a pederast by Vehbi (d. 1809).

From the urban-establishment writers came some remarkable works that incorporate stories from the oral tradition, principally the *Seyahatname,* the massive travelogue and cultural commentary by Evliya Çelebi (d. 1682), and the fascinating *Muhayyelât* (Imaginary Lives) by Aziz Efendi (d. 1798), a collection of three unrelated novellas that amalgamate fantastic tales, novelistic depictions of life in Istanbul, preternatural occurrences, mystical components, and selections from the repertoires of Ottoman professional storytellers.

But Ottoman oral creativity flourished less in written works than on its own terra firma. In the rural areas, it was, along with poetry, music, and dance, a focal performing art. It enchanted everyone from seven to seventy, as the saying goes, at home or at gatherings in villages and small towns. In Istanbul and other major cities, particularly after the mid–sixteenth century, it held audiences captive in coffeehouses; it was a natural expression of the common people, of the man in the street, of the lumpenproletariat who had little else for diversion or entertainment, of the men and women who kept their cultural norms and values alive in giving free rein to their imaginative resources. The leading figures of Ottoman history never ceased to fire the people's imagination. Mehmed "the Conqueror," Prince Cem, Selim "the Grim," Süleyman "the Magnificent," Selim "the Sot," İbrahim "the Mad," Hürrem Sultan (née Roxelana), and Empresses Kösem and Nakşıdil (née Aimée) became mythic names, synonymous with the empire's triumphs and defeats, glories and treacheries. A testament to the popularity of storytelling is the number of terms that identify the various genres within oral narrative: *kıssa, hikâye, rivayet, masal, fıkra, letaif, destan, efsane, esatir, menkıbe, mesel,* and so forth.

The art of the tale was predominantly a continuation of the tradition that the Turkish communities had brought with them from their centuries in Asia. Their shamans from the outset had relied on mesmerizing verses and instructive tales in shaping the spiritual life of the tribes. Tales were at that time talismans and thaumaturgical potions. During the process of conversion to Islam, missionaries and proselytizers used the legends and the historical accounts of the new faith to good advantage.

Storytelling was nurtured also by children's tales told by mothers. In coffeehouses, where the art of storytelling flourished, the *Meddah*s were male professional comics. Their performances offered humorous stories and a broad range of imitations and impersonations. Whereas the *Karagöz* repertoire (notwithstanding its colorful comedic representations of the life of the common people in an urban setting) was relatively fixed in its content, the *Meddah* stories held infinite possibilities of improvisation and originality.

In a society where the rate of literacy remained lower than 10 percent until the mid-1920s, oral narratives played a major role in cultural transmission—hence, the vast corpus of narrative material and the preponderance and success of the short-story genre in recent decades.

Turkish tales are nothing if not fanciful. Most of them contain leaps of the imagination into the realm of phantasmagoria. Even realistic and moralistic stories usually have an element of whimsy. Bizarre transformations abound, as well as abrupt turns of events and inexplicable changes of identity.

The supreme figure of Turkish tales was and remains Nasreddin Hoca, a wit and raconteur who presumably lived in the thirteenth century.[2] A culmination of the earlier tradition, he became the wellspring of the succeeding centuries of folk humor and satire. Popular all over the Middle East, the Balkans, North Africa, and many parts of Asia, he disproves the assumption that one nation's laughter is often another nation's bafflement or boredom. He is Aesop, the Shakespearean clown, Till Eulenspiegel, Mark Twain, and Will Rogers all rolled into one. His humor incorporates subtle irony and black comedy, whimsical observations about human foibles and outrageous pranks, self-satire, banter with God, twists of practical logic, and the outlandishly absurd. But his universal appeal is based always on *ridentem dicere verum.*

Other figures of comic wisdom also appear in folktales, of course: the Ottoman centuries reveled in the humor of Bekri Mustafa, İncili Çavuş, and a host of other comedic characters, including those from the Ottoman minorities. With their irreverence and nonchalance, the Bektaşi dervishes

2. Talat S. Halman has published some of Nasreddin Hoca's stories in English as selected and retold by Aziz Nesin: *The Tales of Nasrettin Hoca* (Istanbul: Dost, 1988).

generated a huge number of quips and anecdotes that have come down through the ages. But Nasreddin Hoca is the humorist par excellence. His universality has been recognized in Europe and America as well. Since the nineteenth century, the Hoca tales have been translated into the world's major languages, primarily English.

Perhaps Nasreddin Hoca's most telling sight gag is the best metaphor for the openness and accessibility of national humor, although initially it might seem forbidding. His tomb in the central Anatolian town of Akşehir originally had walls surrounding it and an iron gate with a huge padlock. In time, the walls came down, but the iron gate with the padlock still stands.

Today, conversations and some types of popular writing in Turkey (and elsewhere) sparkle with Hoca gags or punch lines. The lore has remarkably grown by leaps and bounds through the centuries because much new material has been ascribed or adapted to Nasreddin Hoca by the public imagination.

Since the middle of the nineteenth century, Western narrative traditions have penetrated Turkey at an ever-quickening pace. La Fontaine is a prime example: Şinasi (1826–71), a poet-playwright and a pioneer of Ottoman enlightenment, adapted some of La Fontaine's fables into Turkish verse and composed a few of his own in a similar vein. A century later two great figures, Orhan Veli Kanık and Sabahattin Eyuboğlu, offered their splendid translations of the fables in separate books. Feverish translation activity has likewise contributed to the Turkish synthesis the best of the narrative literature of Europe and America: the Brothers Grimm, Hans Christian Andersen, Perrault, and others in the field of children's tales; Boccaccio, Chaucer, Rabelais, and others in tales for adults. The list is long, and the influences run deep.

Turkish stories—traditional and contemporary—range from simple parables to elaborate stories of quest, from spare narratives to *tekerleme*s, from the heroic deeds of a Turkish Robin Hood to the bizarre doings of jinns and fairies. There are drolleries, cock-and-bull stories, old wives' tales, but also artful stories of psychological insight and spiritual profundity. The versatility is striking: picaresque, picturesque, humoresque, burlesque.

Also, the diversity of tales is quite impressive. Some have elaborate story lines and many layers of meaning; some are so streamlined as to seem puristic. Many possess outright or subtle political criticism, but a few are straight love stories. The action varies from cliff-hangers to the tame. Fatalism alternates with a defiant, almost revolutionary spirit. Many belong to the pure *masal* (tale) genre told for pleasure, whereas some are *mesel* (parables with a moral). In them, we can find dragons, giants, witches, villains, and weird creatures, but also innocent children, lovable characters, romantic lovers, guardian angels. Many tales strike the reader as complete in themselves, commanding quintessential power, but some might well be fragments of an epic or parts of a cycle. The demands on the listener's or reader's mind may be like the suspense of an Agatha Christie thriller, but they can often require one to suspend belief. The vision can change from perfect clarity to trompe l'oeil.

Virtually all tales provide their stimulation through two functions, moral and morale. In this sense, they constitute a strategy for living. For common people oppressed by poverty and other deprivations, they are a diversion, an entertainment, to be sure. *Keloğlan* tales are compelling examples: the Everyboy, who will grow up to be Everyman, proves time and again that the meek—although they might not soon inherit the earth—will endure, sometimes prevail, and at times triumph.

Folktales in the Turkish experience, as elsewhere, are notable not only for their ways of overcoming a weakness or frustration, bringing about the fulfillment of dreams and wishes, and even achieving the impossible, but also for their serving as a continuing critique of and a challenge to entrenched authority, especially against unjust rule. They are not merely a type of *refoulement,* but a form of resistance against tyranny, inequality, or any iniquity. Because most of them possess freedom from time and place, they function in terms of eternal and universal validity. But because they are narrated at a specific moment and locale and are couched in the vocabulary of a particular culture, they have as their targets the symbols of an identifiable society (sultan or vizier, religious judge or feudal lord).

Folktales hold a special place in Turkey's culture and mass communication. Their transcription came much later than comparable work in the West and took place on a much more limited basis. As a consequence, the oral tradition has continued well into our time without becoming frozen on the printed page: it remains alive with new versions and adaptations as well as completely new oral narratives. Even today, despite the intrusions of radio and television, storytelling is alive in many parts of rural Turkey.

Nasreddin Hoca

The thirteenth century was artistically fertile: the Turks of Anatolia proved impressively creative in many genres from the decorative arts to music. In satire, too. A Nasreddin Hoca emerged—wit, raconteur, master of humor. Nasreddin Hoca anecdotes were popular as folk humor, but also in terms of their mystical implications. UNESCO declared 1996–97 "The International Nasreddin Hoca Year."

One of his tales of wisdom is about justice delayed:

One day the Hoca is walking in the bazaar. A thug comes over and slaps him as hard as he can. People run over and apprehend the roughneck. They all go before the judge, who sentences the thug to pay the Hoca one gold coin in damages. The man says: "Your honor, I haven't got a gold coin on me. Allow me to go home and get it." The judge agrees. The Hoca is skeptical. But the judge tells him to sit in the rear of the courtroom and wait for the gold coin. The Hoca doubts if the roughneck will ever show up, but he sits and waits. A couple of hours later, he walks over to the judge: "Your honor," he says, "I've a lot of things to do. I can't wait any longer." The judge insists: "He'll bring the gold coin. Sit down and wait." Another couple of hours pass—no sight of the thug—and the Hoca just can't wait any longer. He slowly gets up, walks over to the judge, slaps him as hard as he can, and says: "When he comes, you get the gold coin."

Occidental Orientation

E UROPE STOOD IN AWE OF THE OTTOMANS, who crushed many states and conquered vast territories, going, as patriotic Turks will proudly point out, "all the way to the gates of Vienna."

The Ottoman Turks, proud of their faith and conquests, felt superior to the West until decline set in. From the seventeenth century onward, there were defeats at the hands of European powers, deterioration of morale and official institutions, and eventually the armed rebellions of the empire's non-Muslim minorities. The Ottoman ruling class gradually became impressed with Europe's growing strength and technological achievements. The Renaissance had wielded no influence on the Turks. The printing press was not introduced to Turkey until the third decade of the eighteenth century, nearly 275 years behind Europe, and the first newspaper in Turkish came out in 1831. The political and ideological impact of the French Revolution was felt decades later, and the Industrial Revolution and its effects eluded the Turks for an even longer time.

By the mid–nineteenth century, the shrinking Ottoman Empire had started to turn to the West for ideas and institutions. After a series of limited innovations in the military, administrative, educational, and technical fields from the eighteenth century on, the Ottoman elite plunged into an extensive transformation usually referred to as "Westernization." In 1839, the Tanzimat (Reforms) Period was ushered in: legal, administrative, and cultural changes were introduced in quick succession. Literature was both a concomitant to and a major catalyst of these changes. The conservative religious establishment waged all-out war against Westernization, however. Cautious reformers recommended a synthesis of Eastern culture and Western technology: *ex Oriente lux, ex Occidente frux.* But progressive intellectuals pressed for extensive changes patterned after European models. The decline of the Ottoman Empire reached a critical point by the middle of the nineteenth century. Younger Turkish intellectuals started seeking the empire's salvation in technological development, political reform, and cultural progress fashioned after European prototypes.[1]

New genres, adopted from Europe, gained ascendancy: fiction, drama for the legitimate stage, journalistic writing, the critical essay, and others. Translations and adaptations accelerated the Europeanization of Turkish literature. Young poets came into contact with European aesthetic theories and values. Although *aruz* was not abandoned, Turkish poets experimented with forms, rhythms, and styles. A reaction began to set in against excessive use of words of Arabic and Persian origin.

Although these ventures and the new genres curtailed the supremacy of verse, poetry was to retain much of its hold over Turkish intellectual life. Particularly at times of social upheaval, it often played a considerably wider and more effective role than many other media.

In the nineteenth and early twentieth centuries, poets were the principal champions of fundamental rights and freedoms—the conveyors of the concepts of nationalism, modernization, social and political reform.

Poetry acquired a social awareness and a political function in the hands of some poets who endeavored to gain independence from external political domination. Ziya Pasha (1829–80), Şinasi (1826–71), and Namık Kemal (1840–88) emerged as literary advocates of nationalism. Recaizade Ekrem (1847–1914) and Abdülhak Hâmit Tarhan (1852–1937) echoed the French romantics. The latter, a prolific poet and author of numerous verse dramas, gained stature as a ceaseless innovator. His poetry covered a wide range of topics and had a philosophic bent as well as a dramatic impact.

The nineteenth-century men of letters inherited the classical and the folk traditions, but they turned their attention to the literary tastes and movements of the West—in particular those of France and, to a lesser extent, England.

---

1. In addition to Bernard Lewis's *The Emergence of Modern Turkey* (London: Oxford Univ. Press, 1966; 3rd ed., 2002), some interesting insights can also be found in Halide Edib (Adıvar), *Turkey Faces West* (New Haven, Conn.: Yale Univ. Press, 1930).

The poetry of the Tanzimat Period and its aftermath had the imperative of revamping its forms, style, and content. It also assumed the task of giving voice to civil disobedience. Its practitioners, despite censorship, often acted as provocateurs and agitators for reform and social innovation and as propagators of rebellion against tyranny.

Poetry became a standard-bearer for such concepts as justice, nation, reform, sovereignty, modernization, freedom, progress, and rights. Şinasi challenged the sultan's absolutism by recognizing Grand Vizier Reşid Pasha as a kind of constitutional authority. Praising Reşit Pasha as a new type of leader, he asked, "Is it any wonder that you are called the apostle of civilization?" and referred to the grand vizier as "the president of the virtuous people." Şinasi assigned a new kind of legislative authority to him: "Your law admonishes the sultan about his limits." Tanzimat poetry also introduced critical views of the Islamic world, as in an excerpt from Ziya Pasha's famous lament:

> In the land of the infidel, I have seen cities and mansions,
> In the dominions of Islam, ruin and devastation.
>
> I have seen countless fools condescend to Plato
> Within the Sublime Porte, that home of divagation.
>
> A traveler on this earth to which we're all condemned,
> I have seen governments and their houses of assassination.
> (Translated by Nermin Menemencioğlu)[2]

Ziya Pasha produced a long satiric poem, many parts of which his contemporaries committed to memory and Turks still widely quote:

> Those who embezzle millions are ensconced in glory
> Those who filch pennies are condemned to hard labor.
>
> . . . .
> How could a uniform make a base fellow noble?
> Put a gold-lined saddle on him, the ass is still an ass.
>
> . . . .
> Pardon is the privilege of the holders of high office;
> Is the penal code used only against the meek?

---

2. *The Penguin Book of Turkish Verse,* edited by Nermin Menemencioglu and Fahir İz (Harmondsworth, U.K.: Penguin, 1978), 164.

The fiction, drama, and journalistic writing of these literary figures were less a substitute for poetry than an extension of it. Their articles and novels were read with greater interest, and their plays had a stronger impact because these writers were, first and foremost, famous poets.

The socially engaged poets of the era launched a consciously utilitarian view of poetry. They fulminated against some of the entrenched Oriental traditions and the repressive Ottoman society. Because of poems of protest or criticism, many poets were penalized and sent into exile.

Tanzimat brought into Turkish poetry a brave new substance—an explicitly formulated political content. Patriotic poets, in particular Namık Kemal, lashed out against the sultan and his oppressive regime. His poems were richly rhetorical pleas for freedom and justice—as in the *kaside* (ode) "To the Fatherland":

> We saw the rulers of the age, their edicts of futility,
> And we retired from office, with honor and with dignity.
>
> From service to their fellow men, true men will never rest,
> The brave of heart will not withhold their help from the oppressed.
>
> A nation may be humbled, and yet not lose its worth,
> A jewel is still precious, though trampled in the earth.
> . . . .
> There is a core of fortitude, the jewel of the heart,
> Which tyranny cannot crush, might cannot tear apart.
>
> How you bewitch us, liberty, for whom so long we strove,
> We who are freed from slavery are prisoners of your love.
>
> Beloved hope of days to come, how warm your presence is,
> And how it frees our troubled world from all its miseries!
>
> Yours is the era that begins, impose your mastery,
> And may God bring fulfillment to all that you decree.
>
> The stealthy dogs of despotism across your homelands creep,
> Awake, O wounded lion, from your nefarious sleep!
>
> (Translated by Nermin Menemencioğlu)[3]

3. Ibid., 167.

The idea of sacrifice, valued highly by the *Divan* poets when done for the loved one, now assumed the form of sacrifice *pro patria:*

> Let fate heap upon me all its torture and pain
> I'm a coward if ever I flinch from serving my nation.

The preceding and following lines by Namık Kemal are typical of the new sense of mission that emerged at the time:

> Let the cannons burst forth and fire and brimstone spread
> May Heaven's gates fling open to each dying comrade
> What is there in life that we should shun falling dead?
>
> — — —
>
> Our greatest joy is to become martyrs in strife
> Ottomans find glory in sacrificing life.

In another poem, Namık Kemal reiterates these themes:

> A soldier's proudest medal is his wound
> And death the highest rank a man can find
> It's all the same beneath or on the ground
> March heroes march and fight to save this land.

Namık Kemal, having established his fearlessness, also gave vent to his fury against the oppressors:

> Who cares if the despot holds an exalted place
> We shall still root out cruelty and injustice.

The great debate in Turkish poetry from the middle of the nineteenth century to the present has centered around the poet's freedom to follow the dictates of his heart and art, as contrasted with his duty to serve his society.

Namık Kemal and Ziya Pasha, who often collaborated in introducing new political and aesthetic concepts, sometimes came into conflict, especially over the extent of the literary changes to be effected. Their friend Şinasi observed: "Ziya and Kemal were both in accord and in opposition—like two forces present in the flash of lightning."

Abdülhak Hâmit Tarhan, often characterized as "the greatest poet of the Tanzimat era," expanded the horizons of Turkish poetry thanks to his erudition in universal culture. He had an excellent private education, formal schooling at the American college (Robert College) in Istanbul; lived for a while in Tehran, where his father was the Ottoman ambassador; then became a career diplomat and served in diverse posts—Paris, Poti (Caucasus), Golos (Greece), Bombay, The Hague, Brussels, and London. His poetry deals with themes of love and nature, death and metaphysics. His verses display mastery of lyric formulation and the philosophical learning of both the East and the West. In his oeuvre, the principle of "art for art's sake" triumphed.

Tevfik Fikret (1867–1915), a prominent poet in later decades, combined in his poetry both the concept of "art for art's sake" and the function of spokesman for protest and civil disobedience. He propagated a novel view of man and society. Standing squarely against the traditional orthodox and mystic conception of man as a vassal to God, he regarded man as having an existence independent of God. Tevfik Fikret placed his faith in reason over dogma, in inquiry over unquestioning acquiescence, in science and technology. He oscillated between romantic agony dominated by despair and an acute social conscience.

He defended the proposition that right is far stronger than might and that the people's rights will ultimately prevail:

> If tyranny has artillery, cannonballs and fortresses
> Right has an unyielding arm and an unflinching face.

In poems that Turks often memorized and circulated clandestinely, Tevfik Fikret lambasted the oppressors:

> One day they will chop off the heads that do injustice . . .
> . . . .
> We have seen all sorts of injustice . . . Is this the law?
> We founder in the worst misery . . . Is this the state?
> The state or the law, we have had more than enough,
> Enough of this diabolical oppression and ignorance.

His assaults on malfeasance and profiteering were equally vehement:

> Eat, gentlemen, eat, this feast of greed is yours,
> Eat till you are fed and stuffed and burst inside out.

At the end of the nineteenth century, when an assassination attempt on the life of Sultan Abdülhamid failed because the sultan's carriage arrived on the spot a minute or two after the planted bomb exploded, Tevfik Fikret in his poem "A Moment's Delay" referred to the would-be assassin as "the glorious hunter" and bemoaned the brief delay:

> The villain who takes pleasure in trampling a nation
> Owes to a moment of delay all his jubilation.

Fikret was a foe not only of the sultan and his henchmen, but also of religious faith and of senseless combat and strife:

> Faith craves martyrs, heaven wants victims
> Blood, blood everywhere, all the time.

Tevfik Fikret bemoaned the sad plight of the declining Ottoman state. In a famous poem entitled "Farewell to Haluk," he reminded his son (Haluk), who was about to depart for university study in Scotland, of the empire's erstwhile glory as well as its ailments:

> Remember when we walked past Topkapı,
> And in a square somewhere along our path
> We saw a plane tree . . . A giant, lifting high
> And wide its branches, its trunk magnificent,
> Proud and unbowed. Perhaps six hundred years,
> Or longer, it had lived its carefree life:
> Spreading its boughs so far, rising so high,
> That all around the city roofs, the domes
> Seemed to prostrate themselves in frozen awe.
> It is the story that our legends tell,
> We see it in the distance, wherever we look.
> But this majestic tree, measuring itself
> Against the sky, is now completely bare—
> Not one green leaf or new bud on its branches.
> It is withering! That deep wound across its trunk,
> Was it the blow of a treacherous ax that fell there,
> The poison of an angry bolt of lightning?
> Proud plane tree, what fire is burning in your heart?
> What somber worms are gnawing at your roots?
> What hands will reach to bind your wound and heal it?
> Who will provide the remedy you need?
> Does the black venom that corrodes your strength

Drip from the ravens circling at your head?
Unhappy motherland, tell us, we ask you,
What evil deeds have caused your suffering?
(Translated by Nermin Menemencioğlu)[4]

In the so-called Constitutional Period, which started after 1876 when the first Ottoman constitution went into effect (although it was abrogated within a few months), Eşref (1847–1912), the most biting and exciting satirist of the time, struck hard at the sultan and his entourage:

O my sultan, this country nowadays is a tree
Its branches get the ax sooner or later.
What do you care if our homeland is lost,
But at this rate you may have no people left to torture.

In a different poem, Eşref states in no uncertain terms:

You are the most vicious of the world's sultans.

Elsewhere he satirizes the Sublime Porte, the seat of Ottoman power:

Everyone's honor and honesty belong to you, my sultan,
So there is no need for either one in your court.

Anatolian poets also bemoaned the current social and economic conditions and leveled strong criticisms at the government. In the nineteenth century, Serdari wrote:

The tax collector rips through the village,
His whip in his hand, he tramples on the poor.

Serdari's contemporary Ruhsatî complained:

There is no justice left, cruelty is all.

Seyrani raised his voice against the merchants' exploitation of the poor people:

Alas, poor people's backs are bent,
We are left to the mercy of commerce.

4. Ibid., 171–72.

But, occasional outbursts of the rebellious spirit in folk poetry aside, it was during the Tanzimat and the Constitutional Period that, for the first time, dissent and outright criticism in poetry for the sake of social and political change became systematic. Unlike in the eras before the mid–nineteenth century, the poets not only lamented social conditions but also advocated revolutionary or evolutionary change to remove them. It is small wonder that the leading poet-rebels of the late nineteenth and early twentieth century who asked for nationhood, constitutional government, basic freedoms, and fundamental rights were persecuted or banished.

Under Sultan Abdülhamid's suppression, most Turkish poets retreated into a fantasy world of innocent, picturesque beauty where, in a mood of meek sentimentality and lackadaisical affection, they attempted to forge the aesthetics of the simple, the pure, and the delectable. Their lyric transformation of reality abounded in new rhythms and imaginative metaphors expressed by dint of a predominantly Arabic-Persian vocabulary and an appreciably relaxed *aruz.* A French-oriented group of poets referred to as *Servet-i Fünun,* after the literary magazine they published, became prominent on the literary scene.

The *Servet-i Fünun* members, enamored of the romantic spirit, represented new directions for the formal and the conceptual process of Turkish poetry. They introduced numerous innovations yet failed to reach a wide audience because of their use of arcane vocabulary studded with words derived from Persian and Arabic.

During the same period, a few minor poets continued *Divan* poetry. Folk poetry, however, maintained much of its vigor and exerted considerable influence on many younger poets striving to create a pervasive national consciousness and to purify the Turkish language by eliminating Arabic and Persian loanwords. Ziya Gökalp (1876–1924), social philosopher and poet, wrote poems expounding the ideals and aspirations of Turkish nationalism. Mehmet Emin Yurdakul (1869–1944) and Rıza Tevfik Bölükbaşı (1869–1949) used folk meters and forms as well as an unadorned colloquial language in their poems.

The short-lived *Fecr-i Âti* (Dawn of Freedom) movement, which stressed both individualistic aesthetics and literature for society's sake, contributed in some measure to the creation of a poetry that Turks could claim as their own.

It is interesting to note that in the first two decades of the twentieth century—a critical phase when the Ottoman state was in its death throes—three rival and occasionally embattled ideologies were publicized by and publicly contested among poets. Tevfik Fikret championed social and governmental reforms, including secularism and Westernization; Mehmet Âkif Ersoy (1873–1936) propagated the Islamic faith as a panacea for the decline of the Ottoman Empire; Ziya Gökalp and Mehmet Emin Yurdakul called for national unity based on the mystique of Turkism and a homogeneous terra firma, a movement that held sway from the early 1910s to around the time the republic was established in 1923 and beyond. The ideology of this so-called Millî Edebiyat (National Literature) benefited from the prodigious talent of Ömer Seyfettin (1884–1920), who produced well-crafted short stories steeped in a patriotic spirit—some of them poignant, and many remarkable for their satiric streak. If he had not died at age thirty-six, he would probably have achieved world-class virtuosity in the genre of short fiction.

Mehmet Âkif Ersoy, a master of heroic diction, devoted much of his verse to the dogma, passion, and summum bonum of Islam. His nationalism has a strong Islamic content, evident in the lyrics he wrote for the Turkish national anthem still sung today. Âkif's elegy "For the Fallen at Gallipoli" is a celebrated expression of the values he upheld:

> Soldier, for these hallowed lands, now on this land you lie dead.
> Your forebears may well lean from Heaven to kiss your forehead.
> How mighty you are, you safeguard our True Faith with your blood;
> Your glory is shared by the braves of the Prophet of God.[5]
> Who could dig the grave that will not be too narrow for you?
> If we should bury you in history, you would break through.
> That book cannot hold your epochs with all their rampages:
> You could only be contained by everlasting ages.
> If I could set up the Kaaba at the head of your pit
> And carve on it the inspiration that stirs my spirit;

5. The original refers to Bedr, a place near Medina where Muslims won a battle in A.D. 624 led by the Prophet.

If I could seize the firmament with all the stars within,
And then lay it as a pall over your still bleeding coffin;
If I could hitch spring clouds as ceiling for your open tomb,
Hang the Pleiades' seven lamps in your mausoleum,
As you lie drenched in your own blood under the chandelier;
If I could drag the moonlight out of night into your bier
To stand guard by you as custodian until Doomsday;
If I could fill your chandelier with dawn's eternal ray,
And wrap your wound at dusk with the sunset's silken glory—
I still cannot say I have done something for your memory.

This pious poet advocated the revival of Islam and had the vision of uniting all Muslims in an Islamic superstate. Yet he made a critical assessment of the backwardness of the Islamic world and proposed a conscientious type of Westernization:

I have spent years wandering in the East,
And I've seen much—not merely idled past!
Arabs, Persians and Tartars, I have seen
All the components of the Muslim world.
I've looked into the souls of little men,
And scrutinized great men's philosophies.
Then, too, what caused the Japanese ascent?
What was their secret? This I wished to learn.
These many journeys, this far-reaching search
Led to a single article of faith.
It's this—
    Do not go far for such a quest,
The secret of your progress lies in you.
A nation's rise comes from within itself,
To imitate does not ensure success.
Absorb the art, the science of the West,
And speed your efforts to achieve those ends,
For without them one can no longer live,
For art and science have no native land.
But bear in mind the warning that I give:

When reaching through the eras of reform,
Let your essential nature be your guide—
There's no hope of salvation otherwise.
(Translated by Nermin Menemencioğlu)[6]

Servet-i Fünun poets—with the singular exception of Tevfik Fikret, who occasionally embraced social causes—preferred subjectivity to such an extent that they were criticized for taking refuge in an ivory tower. Many of them seemed unable to eschew exaggerated emotions, bloated imagery, and overblown language. On the whole, they succeeded in capturing a rather pleasing melodiousness and rhythmic effect even if some of their onomatopoeia seemed strained or superficial. Cenab Şehabettin (1871–1934) was a romantic poet who reveled in lyricism. Committed to formal flexibilities, these poets overcame the rigid styles of most of their predecessors by frequent use of enjambment. Having perfected their use of the sonnet and terza rima, they paved the way for many twentieth-century poets to feel more comfortable about freedom from time-honored stanzaic forms.

The Turkish venture into the realm of European-type fiction started in the 1870s. In the early decades, there was lack of clarity about the basic terms—*short story* or *novella* or *novel?* The pioneering works of fiction came from Ahmet Mithat Efendi (1844–1912), Emin Nihat (d. ca. 1875), and Şemseddin Sami (1850–1904). Of these writers, Ahmet Mithat Efendi, remarkably prolific with scores of novels and collections of short stories he wrote or translated, popularized fiction. Emin Nihat, who died young, produced a single work, *Müsameretname,* a mélange of Boccaccio-like stories, mainly about love and adventure. Şemseddin Sami is generally credited as the author of the first Turkish novel; it deals with the need of schooling for girls and with the problems of arranged marriages.

The prominent poet Namık Kemal produced two novels: *İntibah* (Vigilance), which cautions virtuous people about dissolute living and wicked deeds perpetrated against them, and *Cezmi,* which shows better writing skill and was the first Turkish historical novel. In his only novel, Mizancı Murat (1854–1917), a respected intellectual and historian, gave voice to his critical views of sociopolitical problems and offered the idea of Islamic unity as a panacea. Promising short stories came from Samipaşazade

6. *Penguin Book of Turkish Verse,* 177.

Sezai (1859–1936), whose novel *Sergüzeşt* (1888), about human bondage, introduced the techniques of realism in a firm manner. From Nabizade Nâzım (1862–1893) came the first novella of a Turkish village that heralded naturalism. He also wrote perhaps the earliest specimen of psychological fiction, *Zehra* (published posthumously in 1894), depicting a case of pathological jealousy.

Recaizade Ekrem, a leading poet and litterateur, who also emerged as an important theoretician of aesthetics and a major critic, produced late in his career a satirical novel entitled *Araba Sevdası* (Love for Surrey, 1896), introducing as its protagonist an Ottoman dandy caught in the web of family troubles. This novel successfully caricatured the excesses of Europeanization.

The Ottoman East–West syndrome in the search for European type of reform was perhaps best delineated by Ahmet Mithat Efendi, who assumed for himself the mission of educating the public by dint of literary works. His fiction and essays strove to preserve the best of Islamic values in the Westernizing endeavor of the Ottomans. His 1876 novel with a Europeanized protagonist, Felatun Bey, and a virtuous traditionalist, Rakım Efendi, cautioned modernizers regarding the risk of losing their authentic identity.

Ahmet Mithat Efendi and most of the late-nineteenth-century novelists maintained a utilitarian stance about the function of fiction—mainly to educate readers, to sensitize them concerning the status and rights of women, to create a better social system.

When the ideal of "art for art's sake" gained strength with the establishment of the *Servet-i Fünun* group, the turn of the century witnessed the appearance of the first truly refined Turkish novel, *Aşk-ı Memnu* (Forbidden Love) by Halit Ziya (Uşaklıgil) (1866–1945). This well-constructed novel depicts the life and the tribulations of a prosperous Istanbul family. Its narrative technique is gripping, its story line strong, its characters well delineated, and its dialogue vivid. First serialized in a daily newspaper, it was published in book form in 1900. *Aşk-ı Memnu* can arguably vie with some of Europe's best novels of the time. Halit Ziya authored several other major works, including *Mai ve Siyah* (The Blue and the Black, 1897) and *Kırık Hayatlar* (Broken Lives, 1924), mostly about human suffering.

A year after *Aşk-ı Memnu* appeared on the literary scene, another major talent, Mehmet Rauf (1874–1931), published a psychological tour de force entitled *Eylül* (September, 1901).

Thus, the start of the twentieth century augured well for the Turkish novel, which was destined to take strides toward impressive diversity and workmanship in the ensuing era, eventually culminating in the Nobel Prize.

Attaching themselves to the rising star of fiction, numerous late Ottoman authors—principally Hüseyin Rahmi Gürpınar (1864–1944), Refik Halit Karay (1888–1965), Halide Edib Adıvar (1882–1964), Yakup Kadri Karaosmanoğlu (1889–1974), and Reşat Nuri Güntekin (1889–1956) produced easily readable works whose characters are identifiable and whose dialogues are in the simple vernacular. Güntekin's *Çalıkuşu* (1922; *The Autobiography of a Turkish Girl,* 1949), about a young woman who works in the rural areas as a schoolteacher, became a sensation and remained a best-seller for many decades. Güntekin and the others dominated the fiction of the early decades of the republic as well.

The period from 1859 to 1923 marked the emergence and vigorous evolution of dramatic writing in Turkish. İbrahim Şinasi, poet, author, and translator, wrote the first Turkish play, *Şair Evlenmesi* (*The Wedding of a Poet,*[7] 1860). A few earlier texts by others are probably not original plays, but translations or adaptations from the French. A play that is possibly an original, *Vakaayi-i Acibe ve Havadis-i Kefşger Ahmed* (The Strange Adventures of Ahmed the Cobbler), presumably written in the first half of the nineteenth century by an unidentified author, lacks unassailable authenticity.[8] Şinasi's play, *Şair Evlenmesi,* which was commissioned by the imperial court, is thoroughly Turkish in style, characterizations, dialogue, and dramatic devices. Nüvit Özdoğru, a well-known man of the theater and translator, summarizes the play's basic features:

> A one-act farce, it ridicules the custom of arranged marriages. This was
> a very advanced idea for the Turkey of that period. The play also reveals
> the corruption of some Muslim priests who did business by accepting

7. The English translation by Edward A. Allworth, *The Wedding of a Poet: A One-Act Comedy,* was published in 1981 (White Stone, N.Y.: Griffon House) and reprinted in *An Anthology of Turkish Literature,* edited by Kemal Silay, 240–49, Indiana University Turkish Studies and Turkish Ministry of Culture Joint Series, no. 15 (Bloomington: Indiana Univ. Turkish Studies, 1996).

8. This play was discovered by Fahir İz at the Österreichische Nationalbibliothek in Vienna in 1956. İz published the text under the title *Papuççu Ahmed'in Garip Maceraları* (Istanbul: Yenilik, 1961).

bribes and suggests that people should not blindly follow the priests' teachings. The characters, more types than real persons, spoke in the vernacular of the day. With its broad humor and swift development of theme, the play is not altogether removed from *Karagöz* or *Ortaoyunu*. The form, diction, and the satirical content of the play set the pattern for other playwrights to follow.[9]

With his six plays, Namık Kemal spurred interest in the legitimate stage and dramatic writing. His *Vatan yahut Silistre* (Fatherland or Silistria) is a patriotic play based on an actual event. When it was premiered on April 1, 1873, it aroused enthusiasm and nationalistic excitement. His other plays range in topic from an episode of early Turkic history to the suffering caused by forced marriages to rebellion against tyranny to tragedy in an Indian palace to moral turpitude.

After İbrahim Şinasi's pioneering work, Ahmet Vefik Pasha (1828–91) and Âli Bey (1844–99) offered Molière adaptations; Ali Haydar (1836–1914) and Şemseddin Sami dramatized myths and legends; and Ahmet Mithat Efendi, following in Şinasi's footsteps, turned out many plays exposing the folly of antiquated social mores. These playwrights were acutely aware of their function to educate the public, introduce progressive ideas, criticize social and political institutions, and satirize the types who were responsible for backwardness—for example, the religious fanatic, the bureaucrat, and the rabid conservative.

The closing decades of the nineteenth century, however, were marked by censorship and suppression of works considered dangerous to the sultan and his regime. Plays dealing with revolutionary topics such as strikes, overthrow of government, and uprisings were banned. The mere use of such terms as *freedom, anarchy, dynamite, constitution,* and *equality* could lead to the prosecution of authors and directors.

Under this censorship, innocuous light comedies flourished. Popular taste, too, was a major factor. Molière dominated the scene in nineteenth-century Turkey. Most of his plays were translated or adapted and served as models for scores of new plays by Turkish writers. Molière's principal characters found their counterparts in authentic Ottoman types.

9. Nüvit Özdoğru, "Turkey: Traditional Theater," in *The Reader's Encyclopedia of World Drama,* edited by John Gassner and Edward G. Quinn (New York: Crowell, 1969), 867.

The misers, the misanthropes, and the hypochondriacs—Molière's anti-heroes—became the butt of Turkish satire. The comedy of manners and satirical plays exposing foibles and frailties reached a popularity that was to become pervasive and perennial. Light comedies were characterized by slapstick, clowning, *mal entendu,* horseplay, practical jokes, sight gags, fleecing, infidelity, dialects, and accents.[10]

The earliest specimens of European-style tragedy written by Turkish playwrights made their appearance in the 1860s. The evolution of the genre was to remain under the influence of Racine, Corneille, Shakespeare, and others. Greek tragedy seems to have wielded very little, if any, influence during the last decades of the Ottoman state. But Elizabethan and French tragedy offered nineteenth-century Ottoman playwrights effective models that were assiduously studied and, in some cases, partially plagiarized.[11]

Abdülhak Hâmit Tarhan, one of the dominant figures of Turkish poetry and literary Europeanization, owes much of his fame to the plays he wrote between 1872 and 1918. His early plays were melodramas steeped in sentimentality. Of his twelve tragedies, ten are in classical or syllabic verse either in full or in part. Rhymes and the metric structure give the diction of these plays a forced and contrived quality. The plots are based on intrigue, impossible loves, heroism—all depicted in romantic terms—and are often set in cultures and periods unrelated to the Turkish experience: Assyrian, Arab, Mongolian, Greek, Macedonian, and so on.

The first two decades of the twentieth century were action packed for Ottoman Turkey—domestic strife, independence struggles, limited wars, emergence of a new constitutional regime, party politics, World War I, the Dardanelles campaign, occupations, national liberation. In culture, the period was one of quest, ideological discords, Europeanization versus Islamic traditions. Literature served as the voice of conflicting ideas and ventures.

The Second Constitutional Period, inaugurated in 1908, ushered in freedoms that nurtured literary explorations. While the *Servet-i Fünun*

10. Niyazi Akı, *XIX. Yüzyıl Türk Tiyatrosu Tarihi* (Ankara: Ankara Üniversitesi Basımevi, 1963), 42–43.

11. Although such practices as adaptation without acknowledgment or outright plagiarism were more common in the writing of comedy, careful students of early Ottoman tragedies, in particular Akı, have documented the specific debts to non-Turkish models (Akı, *XIX. Yüzyıl Türk Tiyatrosu Tarihi,* 61–70).

movement stood on its laurels, the *Fecr-i Âti* group introduced new aesthetic principles based mainly on individualism and introspection. The members revealed Parnassian, symbolist, and impressionist influences.

Other notable groups included the *Nev Yunaniler* (Neo-Graecians) poets and novelists, principally Yahya Kemal Beyatlı (1884–1958) and Yakup Kadri Karaosmanoğlu, who incorporated into their work many themes and aesthetic values from the Greek and, to a lesser extent, Roman traditions. Emerging as an alternative and in opposition to the *Nev Yunaniler,* another group embraced the heritage of the entire Mediterranean basin and sought to create a synthesis of the West and the East. They called themselves *Nayiler,* literally "Reed-Flute Players," but figuratively "Virtuosos of Music." Making melodiousness a prime creative asset, they stressed the ideal of "inner harmony" through Yahya Kemal Beyatlı's influence.

The closing decades of the Ottoman state witnessed an abundance of translations and adaptations from Europe. This period was also the heyday of polemics and criticism. With great energy, the stage was set for the revolutions that the young Republic of Turkey would launch.

Republic and Renascence

When the Ottoman state collapsed after nearly 625 years and gave way to the Turkish Republic in 1923, Mustafa Kemal Atatürk devoted his prodigious energies to the creation of a homogeneous nation-state dedicated to modernization in all walks of life, vowing to raise Turkey to the level of contemporary civilization (meaning the West) and higher. In image, in aspiration, in identification, the official and cultural establishment became largely Europeanized. Education was made secular, and reforms were undertaken to divest the country of its Muslim orientation. The legal system adapted the Swiss Civil Code, the Italian Penal Code, and German Commercial Law. Perhaps the most difficult of all reforms, the Language Revolution, was undertaken with lightning speed in 1928, and since then it has achieved a scope of success unparalleled in the modern world. The Arabic script, considered sacrosanct as Koranic orthography and used by the Turks for a millennium, was replaced by the Latin alphabet. This procrustean reform sought to increase literacy, to facilitate the study of European languages, and to cut off the younger generations from the legacy of the Ottoman past. Atatürk also launched a "pure Turkish" movement to rid the language of Arabic and Persian loanwords and to replace them with revivals from old Turkish vocabulary and provincial patois as well as neologisms. Reforms and all, the single common denominator of Turkish identification has significantly been the language. It has provided for social cohesion, cultural continuity, and national allegiance.

Although many of these sweeping reforms did not have a strong impact in the rural areas until the latter part of the twentieth century, in the urban centers drastic changes took place: the political system, religious faith, national ideology, educational institutions and methods, intellectual orientation, daily life, script and language—all underwent transformation. All stages of modern Turkish history (reforms under Atatürk, 1923–38; consolidation under İsmet İnönü, 1938–50; democracy under Adnan Menderes, 1950–60; and the junta, coalitions, caretaker cabinets, parliamentary governments since 1960) have been marked by the thrust of literary modernization.

Today's Turkey is homogeneous in population (more than 99 percent Muslim) and integrated in political and administrative structure, yet it is diversified, full of inner tensions, a battleground for traditionalists versus revolutionaries, fundamentalists versus secularists. In its reorientation, Turkey seems to have traded the impact of Islamic civilization for the influences of Western civilization—at least in the urban areas. During its *vita nuova,* Turkish culture was influenced by Europe, but it was not European as such. It is no longer predominantly Islamic, but it certainly has little kinship with the Judeo-Graeco-Christian world despite the concepts, forms, and values it has adopted from that tradition. It has become a new amalgam of traditions—ancient Turkic, Anatolian, Selçuk, Ottoman, Islamic, Arabic, Persian, European, American—a bridge between two continents, like the two dramatic bridges in Istanbul that now link Europe and Asia. This synthesis, its culture, and literature are enchorial, an original creation of modern Turkey. Whatever the strengths and weaknesses of this synthesis might be, there is no other like it.

Literature was also caught in the maelstrom of reforms. Turkish literature is vibrant with ideologies and the feverish search for values old and new, for styles and tastes, for elements of traditional national culture that may be valid enough to revive, and significant borrowings from the West as well as from other traditions.

In 1923, the influential social thinker Ziya Gökalp wrote: "We belong to the Turkish nation, the Islamic community, and Western civilization. . . . Our literature must direct itself to the people and, at the same time, to the West." His summation of Turkish identity was by and large correct in terms of historical realities and the burgeoning impetus toward Westernization. His counsel for a people's literature that explores the West's literary norms and values proved inspiring and prophetic. The literature of the Turkish Republic has achieved Gökalp's dual objective, but thanks to its versatility it has functioned and achieved impressive accomplishments in other spheres as well.

Revolution, innovation, and Westernization have been the driving forces of the Turkish nation since the beginning of the twentieth century. In the transformation of sociopolitical structure, economic life, and culture, the men and women of letters have served not only as eloquent advocates of progress, but also as catalysts, precursors, pioneers, and creators of brave new ideas. Today, as in the past thousand years, Turkish literature seems to bear testimony to Thomas Carlyle's dictum, "The history of a nation's poetry is the essence of its history: political, scientific, religious," and to Gustave E. von Grunebaum's observation that "literature has always been the art of the Muslim world, masterpieces of painting and architecture notwithstanding."

Poetry or literature in general has been the quintessence of Turkish culture until modern times and a most faithful mirror of socioeconomic realities in Turkey since the inauguration of the republic. Virtually all of the salient aspects of Turkish life, politics, and culture have found their direct or indirect expression in poetry, fiction, and drama, as well as in critical and scholarly writing. The themes and concerns in this literature have included nationalism, social justice, search for modernity, Westernization, revival of folk culture, economic and technological progress, human dignity, mysticism, pluralistic society, human rights and fundamental freedoms, democratic ideals, hero-cult, popular will, Atatürkism, proletarianism, Turanism, Marxist-Leninist ideology, revival of Islamism, humanism—in fact, all aspects and components of contemporary culture.

The function of literature, however, has not been confined to holding up a mirror to society and intellectual life. The basic genres not only have embodied ideas and ideologies, values and verities, beliefs and aspirations but also have served as vehicles of criticism, protest, opposition, and resistance. Literature in Turkey, especially until the last two decades of the twentieth century, has striven to achieve self-renewal in aesthetic terms, to give voice to cultural and socioeconomic innovation, to provide impetus to progressive or revolutionary change, and to serve the cause of *propaganda fide*.

The literary tastes of the republic's early years were dominated by numerous revered poets who had emerged in the twilight of the Ottoman Empire. These prominent figures included Abdülhak Hâmit Tarhan (1852–1937), who, according to E. J. W. Gibb, inaugurated what could be referred to as modern Turkish poetry. He also observed that Tarhan's poems and tragedies in verse made a major impact on the Turkish literary world. Mehmet Emin Yurdakul intoned the mystique of Turkish nationalism: "I am a Turk: my faith and my race are mighty." Ahmet Haşim (1887–1933), under the influence of French symbolists, combined a striking fiery imagery with melancholy sonal effects to create his lyrics of spiritual exile ("We ignore the generation that has no sense of melancholy"), articulated a view that summed up a fundamental aspect of classical poetry, and adumbrated the credo of the neosurrealists of the 1950s and 1960s: "The poet's language is constructed not for the purpose of being understood but to be heard; it is an intermediary language between music and words, yet closer to music than to words." Many of his poems are replete with striking images and metaphors, as in "The Fountain":

> Evening is gathering once again.
>
> My darling laughs at her old place
> Who shuns the daylight and at night
> Above the fountain shows her face.
>
> Girdled by moonlight, now, she stands,
> The sky above her secret veil—
> The stars are roses in her hands.
>
> (Translated by Nermin Menemencioğlu)[1]

In the early part of the republican era, poetry served primarily as a vehicle for the propagation of nationalism. Younger poets branded *Divan* forms and meters as anathema. Native verse forms and syllabic meters gained popularity. Intense efforts were systematically undertaken to purify the language. The group *Beş Hececiler* (Five Syllabist Poets)—Faruk Nafiz Çamlıbel (1898–1973), who was equally adept at *aruz;* Orhan Seyfi Orhon (1890–1972); Enis Behiç Koryürek (1893–1949); Halit Fahri Ozansoy (1891–1971); and Yusuf Ziya Ortaç (1895–1967)—produced simple, unadorned poems celebrating love, the beauties of nature, and the glories of the Turkish nation. Many poets, however, shied away from chauvinism and evolved individualistic worldviews and styles.

---

1. *The Penguin Book of Turkish Verse,* edited by Nermin Menemencioğlu and Fahir İz (Harmondsworth, U.K.: Penguin, 1978), 185.

Neoclassicism gained considerable popularity under the aegis of Yahya Kemal Beyatlı. A supreme craftsman, Beyatlı was a much-acclaimed neo-classicist who produced, in the conventional forms and meters, meticulous lyrics of love, Ottoman grandeur, and the beauties of Istanbul in poems memorable for their refined language and melodiousness. His "Death of the Epicures" is a testament to spiritual tranquility and the aesthetic life:

In the garden of the poet's[2] tomb there's a rose, they say,
Day in day out it blooms anew, its color is blood-choked;
A nightingale weeps all night, they say, till the break of day:
In its tunes, the dreams of the city of love[3] are evoked.

Death for an epicure is the springtime of calm and peace;
For years his soul smolders like incense burning everywhere
While his tomb lies and endures under the cool cypresses—
Each dawn a rose blooms and each night a nightingale sings there.

Nazım Hikmet (1902–63), one of modern Turkey's preeminent poets, famous in his native land and around the world, led the life of a romantic revolutionary. As a teenager, he witnessed the collapse of the Ottoman Empire and lived through the Anatolian upheaval that culmi-nated in the emergence of the Turkish Republic, which he later saw as an anti-imperialist struggle and a class uprising. In 1921, at age nineteen, he went to the Soviet Union to study. He stayed there four years, shar-ing the revolutionary enthusiasm, acquiring ideological orientation, and assimilating literary influences—most notably Mayakovski's verse. After his return to Turkey in 1925, he became a living legend. He published rhythmic, resonant poems of love and justice and sometimes read them before mesmerized crowds in streets and public squares. Theatergoers were eager to see his plays, which were avant-garde in the 1930s not only by Turkish standards, but by European standards as well. Accord-ing to what might be an apocryphal story, he once openly defied Mus-tafa Kemal Pasha (Atatürk), founder of the Turkish Republic. His was a resounding voice of social criticism in the Kemalist age when few dared to say anything unfavorable. He was in and out of prisons on various

2. The poet referred to is Hafiz, a major Persian poet of the fourteenth century.
3. A reference to the Persian city of Shiraz.

Yahya Kemal Beyatlı
(1884–1958)

This poet attained fame for his poems about the metaphysics of life and death.
One of his most famous poems deals metaphorically with death and its aftermath:

Silent Ship

If the day has arrived at last to weigh anchor from time,
A ship departs from this harbor toward an unknown clime.

As if it has no passengers, silently it makes way;
No hand nor handkerchief is waved as it sails away.

This journey is distress for those left behind on the quay,
Their tearful eyes scan the black horizons day after day.

Desperate hearts: This will neither be the last ship to go
Nor the final bereavement of a life filled with sorrow.

In this world, the beloved and the lover wait in vain
Not knowing that the loved ones will never come back again.

Those who sailed away are surely happy with their sojourn:
Years went by since that voyage, yet not one soul will return.

charges between 1928 and 1933, and finally in 1938 he was sentenced—
on what seems, in retrospect, to be unsubstantiated charges—to twenty-
five years in jail. After having served about thirteen of those years, he
was pardoned in 1950. He fled to the Soviet Union in 1951 and spent the
last twelve years of his life writing poetry and doing propaganda stints
in Eastern European countries, Cuba, France, Italy, and elsewhere until
his death in Moscow in 1963.

Nazım Hikmet's artistic life was equally revolutionary: in strictly
aesthetic terms, he introduced or consolidated many new concepts and
techniques whose influence became decisive on modern Turkish poetry.
Among these innovations were free verse, ideological focus, "broken" lines,

organic form, and functional metaphors and images. His poetry created a new blend of lyrical, dramatic, and rhetorical elements. His art was at once utilitarian and poetically motivated. In his best poems, he seemed to have interfused Lorca's spirit with Mayakovski's craft. Nazım Hikmet was truly Turkish and remarkably universal, both a romantic and a rationalist. His vast popularity in Turkey and elsewhere is a testament to a passionate man who cared and dared in everything he did in life and art.

Out of despair and wrath against injustice and exploitation, Nazım Hikmet always offered poetic statements of faith and affirmation, confident "that we'll see beautiful days / we'll see / sunny / days." It is regrettable that simplistic rhetoric rears its head in parts of his massive output, which, at its best, features the lyric and dramatic depictions of the human predicament without reducing it to economic plight.

His earlier poems, which launched free verse in Turkey, put an effusive lyricism at the service of Marxist ideals and made a synthesis of youthful enthusiasm for the machine age, the mystique of a socialist paradise on earth, the rhetoric of journalistic verse, ruthless political satire, and the lyrical outpourings of an incorrigible romantic soul. The later poems, written in and out of prison by an idealist whose spirit was never broken, are often battle cries, but they occasionally betray self-pity and self-dramatization. By 1941, Nazım Hikmet was angry and vengeful: "Our cause / will be fulfilled / alas! / drenched with blood. / And our victory shall be pulled out / like a nail / without mercy." In a poem he wrote in 1931, he described himself as "I, who am an ordinary proletarian poet, / with a Marxist-Leninist conscience."

Nazım Hikmet's masterpiece, *Şeyh Bedreddin Destanı* (*The Epic of Sheikh Bedreddin,* 1977), came out in 1936. It represents the culmination of the best aspects of the poet's art and is remarkably free of its weaknesses. The epic is a lyrical and dramatic account of the uprisings of Şeyh Bedreddin and his followers, including a young revolutionary named Börklüce Mustafa, who in the early fifteenth century founded a religious sect advocating community ownership, social and judicial equality, and pacifism. Nazım Hikmet tells how the Ottoman armies under the command of Royal Prince Murad crushed the uprisings, killed Börklüce Mustafa, and later hanged Şeyh Bedreddin. This work is a perfect synthesis of substance and form, of diction and drama, of fact and metaphor. Bedreddin and Mustafa are treated as tragic heroes whose ideals are thwarted by a cruel death. Fortunately for the poem, Nazım Hikmet's ideological concerns are woven into the action and lyric formulation. An elegiac tone, fully attuned to the historical narrative, precludes the intrusion of the polemics and propaganda that had deleterious effects on Nazım's other major poems. The epic is perhaps the best long poem written in Turkish in the twentieth century.

From: The Epic of Şeyh Bedreddin

It was hot.
The clouds were loaded.
The first drop, like a sweet word, was about to fall.
Suddenly,
        as if pouring from the rocks
                raining down from the sky
                        sprouting out of the soil
like the ultimate creation of this earth,
Bedreddin's warriors confronted the Royal Heir's army.
They were wearing seamless white robes,
        their heads were bare
                feet bare, swords bare.

It was a ruthless battle.

Turkish peasants from Aydın
                Greek sailors from Chios
                   Jewish artisans
Börklüce Mustafa's ten thousand heretical comrades
tore into the forest of enemies like ten thousand axes.
The ranks with red and green banners,
emblazoned shields and bronze helmets
were shattered to pieces
but as the day sank into evening in the torrential rain
the ten thousand were but two thousand.

To sing their songs in unison,
            to drag the nets together out of the water,
            to work the iron together like lace
            to be able to plow the land together

and to eat the honey-filled figs together
to be able to say
            "Together in everything
                    together everywhere
                            except the lover's face"
the ten thousand gave their eight thousand . . .
They were defeated.

The victors wiped the blood off their swords
            on the seamless white robes
                    of the vanquished.
And the earth they had tilled together, with their brotherly hands
like a song sung together
was trampled
            under the hooves of horses bred in the Edirne[4] Palace.

                    * * *

It's drizzling,
fearful,
whispering
like a talk of treason.

Drizzling,
like the patter of the white bare feet of
renegades on damp dark earth.

Drizzling.
In the marketplace of Serez,[5]
across from a coppersmith's shop,
my Bedreddin is hanging from a tree.

Drizzling.
Late on a starless night,
and getting soaked in the rain
swinging from a leafless branch
            is the stark-naked body of my sheikh.

4. Edirne: Adrianopolis, the Ottoman capital of the time.
5. Serez: A small town in present-day Greece.

Drizzling.
The market of Serez is mute,
the market of Serez is blind.
In the air hovers the accursed sorrow of not speaking, not seeing
and the market of Serez has covered its face with its hand.
It's drizzling.

Turkish and non-Turkish men of letters have compared Nazım Hikmet at his best to such figures as Lorca, Aragon, Esenin, Mayakovski, Neruda, and Artaud. No other Turkish poet has been translated into more languages or enjoyed greater acclaim in so many countries. Tristan Tzara, who translated some of Nazım Hikmet's poems into French, paid the following tribute: "The life Nazım led engulfs the experiences of a large segment of mankind. His poetry exalts the aspirations of the Turkish people as well as articulates the common ideals of all nations in humanistic terms."

Nazım Hikmet's most prolific translators into English, Randy Blasing and Mutlu Konuk, have identified him as "the first and greatest modern Turkish poet." He has also earned substantial praise from American and British poets: Denise Levertov affirms, "Nazım Hikmet's poetry, as well as all I have ever heard and read about his life, has always filled me with joy, hope, and new determination towards poetry and struggle"; David Ignatow comments, "He writes our most private thoughts with a zest and love that makes us treasure them in ourselves"; Paul Zweig believes that "Hikmet is one of the few important political poets of this century"; and W. S. Merwin observes, "Hikmet is clearly a figure of great energy and talent."

Although Nazım Hikmet's innovations struck a responsive chord in poetic tastes throughout his life and after his death, they by no means established a monopoly. Most of his contemporaries pursued different courses: Faruk Nafiz Çamlıbel combined neoclassicism with urbanized versions of folk verse; Ahmet Hamdi Tanpınar (1901–62), Ahmet Muhip Dıranas (1908–80), and Ahmet Kutsi Tecer (1901–67) specialized in simple lyrics of genteel sensibilities expressed in tidy stanzaic forms and the traditional syllabic meters.

Ahmet Hamdi Tanpınar followed in the steps of Beyatlı, about whom he produced a sophisticated critical study and whose aesthetics he distilled into crystalline poems written in syllabic verse.

Fear

I have the fear of all the things that end,
I am the Blue Eagle who drags the dawn
Along in his iron beak . . .
                              And life is caught
Within my claws like dangling emeralds
And deathlessness along my lovely swoop
Now bites the thirsty antelope of time.

Ahmet Muhip Dıranas, one of Turkey's best lyric poets, wrote all of his poems in the traditional syllabic meters. His agility in molding his lucid ideas and tender sentiments into these meters is most impressive. So is his ingenuity in finding rhymes.

Two Solitary Trees

Two trees by an odd creek that flows alone
    Stand young strong full-grown;
They have something to say, they do, and yet,
    Dead or alive, they always keep quiet.

After sunset, under the stars, see the way
    The trees sway,
Whatever they have to hold back or declare,
    Dead or alive, it is all laid bare.

By the creek two desolate trees stand
    Pegged onto the ground;
They have something to say, they do, and yet,
    Dead or alive, they have said it—or not.

Necip Fazıl Kısakürek (1905–83), who started out as a poet of romantic agony and spent the latter part of his career as a confirmed Islamic fundamentalist, made an impact with his polished verses, which express suffering as a literary conceit. His major poem "Anguish" stands as a tantalizing poetic examination of the soul's vicissitudes, as evinced by this excerpt:

Month after month I roamed broken, aghast:
My soul was a cauldron that my mind drained;

With the madmen's town one horizon past,
My brain's fantasies were bridled and chained.

Why do all things in the distance dwindle?
In eyeless dreams who gives me piercing sight?
Why the dance of time in the globe's spindle?
I crave wisdom to see my life's twilight.

Thoughts burn as vitriol in the wound's grail
Clinging like leeches to the brain's membranes,
Hail, most majestic of agonies, hail,
Magic log that blooms as it sears and pains.

Asaf Hâlet Çelebi (1907–58) introduced his own iconoclasm in sur-realistic poems that give the impression of somnambulistic writing with intimations of erudition. "A poem," he declared, "is nothing but a long word made up of syllables joined together. Syllables by themselves have no mean-ing. It is therefore futile to struggle with meaning in a poem. . . . Poetry cre-ates an abstract world using concrete materials—just like life itself."

These theories and movements continued to exert varying degrees of influence on the literature of the later decades, but the themes and the tenor of Nazım Hikmet's verse probably had the widest impact. Effective voices were raised among poets, dramatists, fiction writers, essayists, and journalists against the established order and its iniquities, oppression of the proletariat, and national humiliation suffered at imperialist hands. The poetry of social realism concentrates on the creation of a just and equitable society. It is often more romantic and utopian than rhetorical, containing sensual strains, tender sentiments, and flowing rhythms, but also occa-sionally given to invective and vituperation.

One of Turkey's earliest progenitors of free verse was Ercüment Behzad Lâv (1903–84). Ahmet Oktay (b. 1933), an astute critic, defined Lâv's aesthetic strategies as "surface modernism"—an observation that has considerable validity in view of the fact that Lâv was virtually an innovator for innovation's sake. There are few affirmations in what he wrote, little of what made other poets appealing to those who seek pleasure, and certainly none of the easy communicability of the ideological rhetoric that turned some of his contemporaries into heroes. One tends to concur with the bril-liant scholar-critic Orhan Burian (1914–53), who observed in the late 1940s that Lâv is "committed to the cause of creating a new type of poetry out of half-baked ideas and hidden sound structures." "There is a dryness in his poems," Burian continued. "His short poems, which give voice to momentary emotions, are more attractive."

Cahit Sıtkı Tarancı (1910–56), an accomplished master of syllabic verse, expressed simple sentiments distilled into exquisite yet sometimes excruciating lines. One of his best poems, "After Death," is a chilling lyric of shattered faith in life and in life after death:

With many hopes about death we perished,
But the charm was broken in a vacuum.
Our song of love we cannot help exhume,
A view of the sky, tuft of twigs, bird's plume;
Living was a habit we had cherished.

No news comes from the world now or ever;
No one misses us, no soul cares to know,
The darkness of our night is endless, so
We might just as well do without a window:
Our image has faded from the river.

One of modern Turkey's most popular poets, Cahit Külebi (1917–97), has as the hallmarks of his art a sensuous, sentimental involvement in human experiences, an admiration for ecological beauty, an infatuation with life's simple joys, and a lucid style that revels in the colors and rhythms of the Turkish vernacular.

A Tiny Spring

I am a tiny spring
On a forsaken mountain
My waters will never cease
I shall keep flowing
Under the starlight on and on.

Travelers don't hear my voice
As they go by night and day.
From this parched land and burning hearts
This thirst will never go away.
All our longing will forever stay.

There are times when animals come near
And drink their fill of my waters.
What do beasts know of this flavor.
Still, their eyes are full of glitters.
All my days go by this way.

Sometimes a seed falls into my waters.
Hold it, my neighboring soil, embrace it!
O seed, powerful seed, sprout at once,
Let your roots strike deep into the earth
To grace it.

I'm a tiny spring, what do I care?
I shall never despair.

A frontal thrust for modernization took place in the early 1940s when
Orhan Veli Kanık (1914–50), Oktay Rifat (1914–88), and Melih Cevdet
Anday (1915–2002) launched their "Poetic Realism" movement. Their urge
for literary upheaval was revolutionary, as expressed in a joint manifesto
of 1941 that called for "altering the whole structure from the foundation
up . . . dumping overboard everything that traditional literature has taught
us."[6] The movement did away with rigid conventional forms and meters,
reduced rhyme to a bare minimum, and avoided stock metaphors, sten-
torian effects, specious embellishments. It championed the idea and the
ideal of "the little man" as its hero, the ordinary citizen who asserted his
political will with the advent of democracy. Kanık's "Epitaph I" is precisely
this type of celebration:

He suffered from nothing in the world
The way he suffered from his corns;
He didn't even feel so badly
About having been created ugly.
Though he wouldn't utter the Lord's name
Unless his shoe pinched,

---

6. The manifesto was published at the beginning of Orhan Veli Kanık, *Garip* (Istan-
bul: Resimli Ay, 1941). An English translation is given in Talat S. Halman, "Introduction,"
in *I Am Listening to Istanbul: Selected Poems of Orhan Veli Kanık* (New York: Corinth,
1971), xiv–xv.

He couldn't be considered a sinner either.

It's a pity Süleyman Efendi had to die.

The *Garip* (Strange) Group, as the Kanık–Rifat–Anday triad is referred to, endeavored to write not only *about* the common man, but also *for* him. In order to communicate with him, they employed the rhythms and idioms of colloquial speech, including slang. With their movement (later dubbed "The First New" movement), the domination of free verse, introduced in the 1920s by Nazım Hikmet, became complete. They proclaimed with pride: "Every moment in the history of literature imposed a new limitation. It has become our duty to expand the frontiers to their outer limits, better still, to liberate poetry from its restrictions."

Many of Kanık's poems are frequently quoted by Turks, a favorite one being the three-line poem entitled "For Our Homeland":

All the things we did for this land of ours!

Some of us died;

Some of us gave speeches.

Orhan Veli Kanık presided over this demise of strict stanzaic forms and stood squarely against artifice, hackneyed metaphors, and a variety of clichés and literary embellishments that had rendered much of Turkish poetry sterile. His poems deal with everyday life expressed in direct terms. Although the use of free verse had been established earlier, it was Orhan Veli who made *vers libre* and the French modernists relevant to contemporary Turkish poetry. His iconoclasm paved the way for a poetry steeped in the vernacular and stripped of adornments. By liberating his contemporaries from the stultifying weight of the past, he made them conscious of the life and values of Everyman. Any and all topics could be treated poetically, and poets were free to use all the expressive resources of the Turkish language.

Orhan Veli's first book, *Garip* (1941), which included the work of his best friends Oktay Rifat and Melih Cevdet Anday, was also his most controversial and influential. Their joint manifesto with which it begins was influenced, according to Oktay Rifat, by André Breton's *Manifeste du surréalisme* and marked a turning point in the modernization of Turkish poetry. It declared:

The literary taste on which the new poetry will base itself is no longer the taste of a minority class. People in the world today acquire their right to life after a sustained struggle. Like everything else, poetry is one of their rights and must be attuned to their tastes. This does not signify that an attempt should be made to express the aspirations of the masses by means of the literary conventions of the past. The question is not to make a defense of class interests, but merely to explore the people's tastes, to determine them, and to make them reign supreme over art.

We can arrive at a new appreciation by new ways and means. Squeezing certain theories into familiar old molds cannot be a new artistic thrust forward. We must alter the whole structure from the foundation up. In order to rescue ourselves from the stifling effects of the literatures which have dictated and shaped our tastes and judgments for too many years, we must dump overboard everything that those literatures have taught us. We wish it were possible to dump even language itself, because it threatens our creative efforts by forcing its vocabulary on us when we write poetry.

There are no stentorian effects in Orhan Veli's verse, no rhetoric, no bloated images. In most of his poems, he strikes a vital chord by offering the simple truth, and he is usually so sincere as to seem almost sentimental. He never wrote a complex line or a single perplexing metaphor. His verse was a purist's revolt against facile meters, predetermined form and rhythm, pompous diction. Style, in his hands, became a vehicle for the natural sounds of colloquial Turkish.

In a poetic career that spanned half a century until his death in 1988, Orhan Veli's friend Oktay Rifat also stood at the vanguard of modern Turkish poetry—first as an audacious, almost obstreperous rebel, then as an eclectic transformer of styles and language who was writing from a self-enforced privacy, and finally as a reclusive elder statesman who was creating a unique synthesis. One could say that these three stages in his writing correspond roughly to movements elsewhere in world literature— the socialist surrealism of the 1930s and 1940s; the obscurantism of the French poets Apollinaire, Supervielle, Aragon, Éluard, Soupault, and Prévert; and, finally, what one can only call "pure poetry."

Oktay Rifat's poetry is in fact unique—the result of a very personal development. It defies critical analysis in terms of literary schools or influences. Although in the early phase of his career he seemed to belong to an emerging school, he stood squarely against any school that confined a poet's aesthetic taste. In 1941, when he became a member of *Garip,* he insisted that the text of the manifesto include the following statement: "The idea of literary schools represents an interruption or pause in the flow of time. It is contrary to velocity and action. The only movement that is harmonious with the flow of life and does not thwart the concept of dialectics is the 'no-school movement.'"

Although most of his output from the mid-1960s on was either spontaneously or consciously universal, Rifat occasionally returned to Ottoman history. In a number of poems, he evokes Byzantium and the Ottoman Empire in masterful terms. He remarkably utilizes for most of these poems the sonnet form and some light rhymes. The synthesis becomes more encompassing with fascinating returns to roots, not the least of which is that his surprising turns of phrase and paradoxical concepts have their parallels in his predecessors' imagination. One is reminded of a famous poem by the Anatolian mystic Yunus Emre (d. ca. 1321), which has such lines as

> I climbed to the branches of a plum tree,
> And I helped myself to the grapes up there.
>
> I snatched one of the wings of a sparrow
> And loaded it onto forty ox-carts.
>
> The fish climbed the poplar tree
> To gobble the pickles of tar up there.

A folk saying goes as follows: "The water buffalo built its nest on a willow branch." Rifat sometimes echoed this verbal imagination.

"I am," wrote Melih Cevdet Anday, the third member of the *Garip* triumvirate, in an early poem, "the poet of happy days." This was the tongue-in-cheek, sardonic opening line of a poem entitled "Yalan" (Lies), which laments that life's cruelties make it impossible for a poet to bring beauty and good tidings to his people. From his first appearance on the Turkish literary scene in 1936 until his death in 2002, Anday felt this ironic frustration as he oscillated between the poetry of commitment to social causes and pure poetry. His earliest poems were simple romantic sentimental lyrics. From the early 1940s until the late 1950s, he wrote for and about the oppressed man in the street, protesting social injustice.

I Am Listening to Istanbul

I am listening to Istanbul, intent, my eyes closed:
At first there is a gentle breeze
And the leaves on the trees
Softly sway;
Out there, far away,
The bells of water-carriers unceasingly ring;
I am listening to Istanbul, intent, my eyes closed.

I am listening to Istanbul, intent, my eyes closed;
Then suddenly birds fly by,
Flocks of birds, high up, with a hue and cry,
While the nets are drawn in the fishing grounds
And a woman's feet begin to dabble in the water.
I am listening to Istanbul, intent, my eyes closed.

I am listening to Istanbul, intent, my eyes closed.
The Grand Bazaar's serene and cool,
An uproar at the hub of the Market,
Mosque yards are full of pigeons.
While hammers bang and clang at the docks
Spring winds bear the smell of sweat;
I am listening to Istanbul, intent, my eyes closed.

I am listening to Istanbul, intent, my eyes closed;
Still giddy from the revelries of the past,
A seaside mansion with dingy boathouses is fast asleep.
Amid the din and drone of southern winds, reposed,
I am listening to Istanbul, intent, my eyes closed.

I am listening to Istanbul, intent, my eyes closed.
A pretty girl walks by on the sidewalk:
Four-letter words, whistles and songs, rude remarks;
Something falls out of her hand—
It's a rose, I guess.
I am listening to Istanbul, intent, my eyes closed.

I am listening to Istanbul, intent, my eyes closed.
A bird flutters round your skirt;
On your brow, is there sweat? Or not? I know.
Are your lips wet? Or not? I know.
A silver moon rises beyond the pine trees:
I can sense it all in your heart's throbbing.
I am listening to Istanbul, intent, my eyes closed.

Orhan Veli Kanık (d. 1950)

After their innovations of the 1950s ground to a halt, both Oktay Rifat and Melih Cevdet Anday abandoned their earlier insistence on simplicity, the vernacular, concrete depiction, epigrammatic statement, and so on, which had been the hallmarks of the *Garip* group. Oktay Rifat took up a fertile type of neosurrealism, proclaiming that "poetry tells or explains nothing because beauty explains nothing." He produced subtle abstract poems, some of which are notable for intellectual architectonics, mostly devoid of social or political engagement. Anday's work moved toward lucid philosophical inquiry: his new aesthetic formula was, in his own words, "thought or essences serving as a context for arriving at beauty." His long poems of the 1960s and 1970s—*Kolları Bağlı Odysseus (Odysseus Bound)*, "Troya Önünde Atlar" ("Horses at the Trojan Gates," also published as "Horses before Troy"), *Göçebe Denizin Üstünde (On the Nomad Sea)*—sought a synthesis of universal culture and endeavored to construct superstructures of ideas, myths, and legends. Although he never abandoned his humanism, his affirmation of life, and his lucid diction, everything else about his poetry—substance, style, syntax—changed radically. His final break with his past came with the 1962 publication of *Kolları Bağlı Odysseus*, a long poem consisting of four parts that might well be Anday's magnum opus. In it, his preoccupation is not with social causes, but with modern man's philosophical predicaments. Here Anday avoids the stark-naked style and explores expressive resources precisely attuned to the complexities of human existence. Deviating from his concept of man as a cog in the unjust and heartless wheel of society, he adopts *Homo sapiens* as his hero. Claiming Odysseus as his aggrandized Everyman and leaving Homer alone until the fourth and last part, Anday creates a modern universal mythology. This cerebral work, one of the few excellent long Turkish poems written in the twentieth or any other century and certainly a landmark in Turkish philosophical poetry, shows a piercing mind.

In the late 1950s, a strong reaction set in against "Poetic Realism." Literature of commitment came under fire in some circles. This response is reflected in "Poetry Lesson" by Salâh Birsel (1919–99):

Take "Love for Mankind" as your topic
And free verse as prosody.
Relevant or not,
Whenever it occurs to you,
Insert the word "hunger"
At a convenient spot.
Near the end of the poem
Rhyme "strife" with "the right to good life."
There—that's the way to become a Great Poet.

Behçet Necatigil (1916–79) was Turkey's foremost intellectual poet who enjoyed a well-deserved reputation for his subtle, indefatigably inventive poems. Necatigil severed himself from sentimental romanticism, which was the umbilical cord to all his predecessors and most of his contemporaries. He carried depersonalization farther than any Turkish poet and banished all subjective intrusions, value judgments, didacticism, and moralizing from his poetry. Necatigil made poetry itself reign supreme. He regarded all things and all phenomena as being possible or at least plausible. This approach granted him the freedom to look beyond the physical state and enabled him to discover distant and seemingly paradoxical relationships among objects, actions, emotions, and concepts.

This brand of poetry is not allied with surrealism; Necatigil never strayed from the plane of consciousness. Nor is it akin to symbolism, for he used no symbols with traceable referents. Nor is it "poetry of abstraction" à la Paul Valéry or Wallace Stevens because it does not distill essences or recognize abstraction as the supreme reality. The term *obscurantist* does not apply, either: for all his opaque references and unidentified insights, Necatigil made no effort to forge an aesthetics of the obscure. One might call his poetry "Cubism" and his creative approach "extraspection." He consciously explored external reality, disintegrated it, and then, out of the disjointed ingredients, re-created a new synthesis. His art derived its creative energy from transforming visions and revisions of reality.

Necatigil is among the few independent poets who refused to be pigeonholed. Uncompromising in his aesthetic views, he stands unique. His poetry has a shape and a voice unlike anyone else's. No other Turkish poet is so thoroughly original or so staunchly individualistic.

He may well be to Turkish poetry what Wallace Stevens has been to American poetry, although there is virtually no resemblance between them in terms of style or substance. It is futile to look for influences when analyzing the basic features of Necatigil's art. He may have found a few themes and devices in the stark abstractions of post–World War II German poetry, but they are subtle and elusive, as is his entire poetic approach.

Necatigil's "intellectual complexity" is a functional creative process that starts with visual and conceptual concentration on an object or phenomenon, places it into a web of distant relationships, distills from it the ultimate abstractions, and expresses it in terms and idioms that stretch the resources of the language to its outer limits. No single poetic voice in modern Turkey is as spare and esoteric or as precise in expressing a vision or a speculation. Although Necatigil is the modern poet par excellence, his creative strategy, based as it was on the proposition that language is the supreme intellect, tends to reaffirm the aesthetic values of classical Ottoman poetry, about which he was fully knowledgeable. Verbal richness, subtle imagery, assonances, visions, and abstractions—the ultimate values of Turkey's bygone poetic tradition—find their ultramodern *vita nuova* in Necatigil's work. His poetry reconstructs the external world as well as the world of imagination through the prospects of language. He proves, by means of his explorations, that poetry can re-create both our inner and our outer life.

In the mid–twentieth century, an energetic new movement emerged often identified as *İkinci Yeni,* "The Second New." İlhan Berk (1918–2008), perhaps Turkey's most daring and durable poetic innovator, acted as spokesman for the movement, especially at the outset, pontificating: "Art is for innovation's sake." Berk's aesthetics occasionally strove to forge a synthesis of Oriental tradition and Western modernity. In his *Şenlikname* (The Festival Book, 1972), for instance, he conveys through visual evocations, old miniatures, engravings, and subtle sonorities the vista of Ottoman life and art; yet the poetic vision throughout the book is that of a modern man, neutral rather than conditioned by his culture, in a sense more European than Turkish. Berk is the most protean of Turkey's modern poets. In the 1930s, he launched his career with smooth, mellifluous lyrics, but in the 1940s he became socially engaged and produced many excellent verses that were stark in their realism. By the mid-1950s, he had published *Köroğlu,* one of modern Turkey's best adaptations of folk themes. He was soon afterward in the vanguard of obscurantism, of which he produced several notoriously extreme specimens.

From the 1940s to the early 1960s, Berk often exposed his art to the impact of contemporary French poetry. In the mid-1960s, he announced his resounding departure from European influences and embraced the norms and values of Turkish classical poetry. *Âşıkane* (double entendre: Like a Lover or Like a Minstrel, 1968) embodies the last group of Berk's French-oriented sonnets and his first collection of verses with a classical flavor. The lyrics in the latter category are in the form and spirit of the *gazel,* which was the most popular verse form in Islamic Middle Eastern literatures.

Berk's aesthetics later strove to forge a synthesis of visual art and sound effects, of spatial and temporal realities, of history and man's higher consciousness. On a different level, it created admixtures of the past and the present, and cultural fusions of Oriental tradition with Western modernity. One of his best-known poems idealizes love:

Love

When you were here we never knew such a thing as evil
Life had neither mishaps nor these dark griefs
Without you they put hope on the line of gloom
Without you they scratched out our happiness
For a long time now the sea doesn't look lovely from the window
For a long time now we lack human life because you're gone.
Come lead us into new ages.

The forms and values of classical poetry, too, were kept alive by a group of highly accomplished formalists who clustered mainly around the monthly *Hisar,* which ceased publication in 1980 after thirty years.

Among the daring and quite impressive explorations into Turkey's own literary heritage have been those undertaken by Turgut Uyar (1927–85),

Attilâ İlhan (1925–2005), and Hilmi Yavuz (b. 1936); the latter remains at the forefront of modern innovators who absorbed and revitalized many of the salient features of classical aesthetics, Islamic culture and beliefs, and traditional Turkish values.

From: the dig

poems must be dug into: you supposed
i saw the manuscript
with its crimson rubrics
buried by those delicate exiles
you found heart-broken papers
their sorrow frozen, leathern their ashes
    and suddenly,
as their pain touched your pain
        (Translated by Walter G. Andrews)[7]

Although these three major figures are highly individualistic and their works drastically different from one another, they all have acknowledged the need for coming to terms with the viable and valuable aspects of the Ottoman-Turkish elite poetry. They have used not its stringent forms and prosody, but its processes of abstracting and its metaphorical techniques.

Much of Turgut Uyar's output has conveyed a sense of discontent, if not disgust, with humanity and a firm conviction of man's inherent evil, which Uyar seems to blame—in poetic rather than moral terms—for the past vicissitudes of human history and for its present tragic state. Human society, according to his work's basic philosophical premise, is bent on destroying itself: it inflicts conflagrations upon itself and rejoices in the ashes. Yet miraculously it arises, phoenixlike, out of those ashes to perpetuate its existence, albeit in near chaos and in banishment from immortality. Aesthetically, Uyar has a sharp aptitude for recognizing bad habits in creative efforts—in particular, his own.

---

7. Hilmi Yavuz, *Seasons of the Word,* translated by Walter G. Andrews (Syracuse, N.Y.: Syracuse Univ. Press, 2007), 40.

Quiet reflection alternates with eruptions of anger and nausea, moves on to nightmarish abstract depictions, then resolves itself into an ontological probe wherein Uyar masterfully fuses the concrete and abstract elements of reality.

At its best, Uyar's poetry is a well-wrought blend of senses and action with ingenious metaphor. In "Terziler Geldiler" (And Came the Tailors), which is arguably one of the best poems of his entire career, he achieves a summation of creation and its attendant anarchy: life's warp and woof constantly restoring itself and disintegrating into death. It is a theme of Herculean dimensions, and Uyar does justice to it by eliciting meaningful abstract formulations out of an imaginative juxtaposition of images, allusions, and philosophic lunges into the diverse aspects of reality. Death became dominant in Uyar's poetry as a concomitant of his pessimism. He was preoccupied with death as the inescapable end and therefore as an end in itself: in "Övgü, Ölüye" (In Praise of the Dead), he evokes death's sundry aspects by dint of perhaps the most striking delineation of a corpse in all of Turkish literature.

Uyar's line "on the shore of all possibilities" sums up the dysfunctional aspects of this new esoteric poetry, which is marked by such wild thrusts of imagination and distortion of language that some critics denounced it as "word salad." "Vanish," by Edip Cansever (1928–86), is one of the prime examples (the first two stanzas quoted here):

I reiterate your face is a laughter
Glance and an armada of life marches into light
A flower that hails from subterranean regions
An eagle gone stark-naked
Now pink is pursued by three persons
Upward along your shoulders
Drive them insane in your hair
Carnation multiple
Carnation shrinking shrunk

Most beauty arises in your most secret places
Lovely as animals suddenly born
Glance and I deliver a poem to the world
A poem is made red round wide

Widest reddest on planes oppressed
A secret is now pursued by three persons
Inward along your eyes
Drive them insane in my lines
Carnation divided
Carnation multiplied multiple

Attilâ İlhan, Turkey's most successful neoromantic poet as well as a major novelist and essayist, attempted to recapture the milieu and moods prevailing during the slow death of the Ottoman Empire. Known also as a creator of imaginative and touching love poems, he introduced a vigorous new style, as evidenced in "Ancient Sea Folk," quoted here in part:

pebbles chant an odd song there and the sea shepherds
drive their herds into the high seas
while on the mussels' iris harlot blues crouch
in the boundless western time's green galleons
unforgettable and emerald and sighted
blood-drenched slab by slab
you hear the ancient sea folk in harbor taverns
those kinky sea people if you listen
spanish songs and italian wine
and godlike you create curses
from fifteen meridian to twenty you create universal curses
atop the mainmast
you god of blasphemy and tumult and of my enigma
you god of lost treasures
you shall not look behind nor spit at the wind
unless black flags are hoisted on the admiral's mast
no honest breeze shall spark your corsair's eyes
unless you chew on the rain or on tobacco

I never forgot the mediterranean
I plunged into flames and wept voraciously
the joy of creating
and being created flared tremulously in the sky
and prayers burst open like titanic sails

then lo and behold three crescents arose at once
barbarossa[8] songs released like hawks from their arms
cyclone-sized barefoot mariners of the algerian skipper
who arrested the caravans of ships
and held the straits of messina and septe and all others
there is no god but God

This type of self-serving aestheticism represents a "supreme fiction" at its best and sterile confusion at its worst. A leading critic, Rauf Mutluay, deplores its egocentricity and narcissism as "the individualistic crisis and this deaf solitude of our poetry." The language is usually lavish; the poetic vision is full of inscapes and instresses; ambiguity strives to present itself as virtuosity; metaphors are often strikingly original but sometimes run amuck. Euphuistic and elliptical writing is a frequent fault committed by the practitioners of abstract verse. The best specimens, however, have an architectonic splendor, rich imagination, and human affirmation.

In obscurantism, the critic Memet Fuat finds the malaise of the age, calling it "the critique of the time we live in—the poems of individuals who are oppressed, depressed, and shoved into nothingness." The poet Edip Cansever calls for, as a principle of the new aesthetics, the "death of the poetic line," whose integrity had been accepted as a fundamental artistic value for generations of Turkish poets: "The function of the poetic line is finished." Extending this statement to the self-imposed isolation of the obscurantists, Mutluay speculates that "perhaps the function of poetry is finished." Cansever's poetic vision is afflicted with that modern malaise that divines man's obsolescence and focuses its energies on pain and grief in the face of his unheroic existence. Cansever occasionally expresses this *mal du siècle* in simple lyric lines—for example: "our hearts are a dilapidated monastery" or "it is a poet's face that bleeds from loneliness / a face as elongated as days without women." However, he often prefers the unusual but meticulous metaphor, which characterizes the better work of Turkey's so-called "The Second New" movement—a school with which Cansever had been affiliated from the beginning of his career.

8. "Barbarossa" Hayreddin Pasha: Admiral of the Ottoman fleet in the reign of Sultan Süleyman the Magnificent (sixteenth century).

Cemal Süreya (1931–90), a major figure of "The Second New" started out in the mid–twentieth century with bold innovations, wild thrusts of imagination, and distortions of language. In time, he would move away from the esoteric to the lucid.

Rose

Seated at the core of the rose I weep
As I die in the street each night
Ahead and beyond all unmindful
Pang upon pang of dark diminution
Of eyes upheld blissful with life.

Your hands are in my caress into dusk
Hands forever white forever white
Cast into my soul icicles of fright
A train stays at the station for a short while
A man who sometimes can't find the station that's me.

On my face I rub the rose
Fallen forlorn over the pavement
And cut my body limb by limb
Bloodgush doomsday madmusic
On the horn a gypsy is reborn.

Cemal Süreya's eloquent lines, written in 1966, embody the revolutionary experience, the disorientation as well as the optimism and the stirring search of the "New Turkey":

We are the novices of new life
All our knowledge is transformed
Our poetry, our love all over again
Maybe we are living the last bad days
Maybe we shall live the first good days too
There is something bitter in this air
Between the past and the future
Between suffering and joy
Between anger and forgiveness.

Ece Ayhan (1931–2002), a confirmed maverick from his emergence in the 1950s on, was a member of "The Second New." He championed *anlamsız şiir,* meaningless or absurd poetry. The best of this brave new poetry has as its hallmarks vivid imagination, an enchanting musical structure, and an intellectual complexity that dazzles with its audacious metaphors.

Most of "The Second New" poets marched toward clarity. But Ece Ayhan chose arcanum. Every element of his poems became esoteric, oblique, indecipherable. In syntactical difficulties and inaccessible allusions, few poets came close to the challenges Ayhan posed. Readers and critics have racked their brains to make sense of the surface problems as well as the unfathomable secrets.

One of Ayhan's intriguing books is *Orthodoxies,*[9] where underneath the ambiguities there are subtle and often sly symbols, most of which deal with minority cultures—"the nigger in the photograph," "the secret Jew," "Ipecacuanha the Emetic," Mistrayim, Armenians, the Greek and Russian Orthodox.

Many degrees of separation lend Ayhan's poetry its fascination and sardonic fury. There is much clash of cultures and sects here, but the tragic core is constituted by homosexual culture, declared anathema by hypocritical public mores.

In sharp contrast to urban elite litterateurs, village poets, standing *media vitae,* serve their rural communities by providing enlightenment as well as live entertainment. The minstrel tradition, with its stanzaic forms and simple prosody, is alive and well. Particularly since the 1950s, many prominent folk poets have moved to or made occasional appearances in the urban areas. Âşık Veysel (1894–1973), a blind minstrel, produced some of the most poignant specimens of the oral tradition.

> I walk on a road long and narrow:
> Night and day, on and on I go.
> Where am I heading? I don't know:
> Night and day, on and on I go.
>
> Even in sleep I must forge ahead:
> No rest for the weary, no warm bed;

9. Ece Ayhan, *Ortodoksluklar* (Istanbul: De, 1968); *A Blind Cat Black; and, Orthodoxies,* translated by Murat Nemet-Nejat (Los Angeles: Sun and Moon, 1997).

Fate has doomed me to the roads I dread.
Night and day, on and on I go.

Who can tell why my life went awry?
Sometimes I laugh, sometimes I cry.
Craving a caravanserai,
Night and day, on and on I go.

Âşık Veysel
(1894–1973)

The Turkish minstrel is referred to as âşık—*meaning both "lover" and "folk poet." Popular belief is that the poet is a man of love: love of beauty, of God, of nature, of the nation, of justice, of humanity. Âşık Veysel uttered the eloquence of love. "Love and passion and the loved one are all in me" was his declaration of all-embracing love. Like his mystic predecessors, he proclaimed: "God's existence is embedded in Man."*

He expressed his profound devotion to his country in the following two memorable lines:

> *You are closer to me than myself.*
> *I would have no life if you did not exist.*

This Turkish Muslim folk poet was a humanist with boundless religious tolerance and an ecumenical vision:

> *The Koran and the Bible are God's grace*
> *Which is what all four holy books embrace;*
> *To scorn and segregate this or that race*
> *Would be the darkest blemish on one's face.*

He made a plea for universal brotherhood and unity:

> *Come, brother, let us unite in harmony.*
> *Let us love each other like brothers, heart to heart.*

Many Turkish poets were absorbed by a concern for world affairs. Their motivation was ideological or humanistic; nonetheless, they commented on international events with telling effect. They poured out elegiac poems for John F. Kennedy, Martin Luther King Jr., Ho Chi Minh, and Salvador Allende, along with indictments of the war in Vietnam, celebrations of man's conquest of the moon, and moving accounts of the tragedies of Algeria, Cyprus, Palestine, and elsewhere.

The most encompassing poetic achievement of contemporary Turkey belongs to Fazıl Hüsnü Dağlarca (1914–2008), the winner of the Award of the International Poetry Forum (Pittsburgh) and the Yugoslav Golden Wreath (Struga), previously won by W. H. Auden, Pablo Neruda, and Eugenio Montale and later by Allen Ginsberg and others. His range is bewilderingly broad: metaphysical poetry, children's verse, cycles about the space age and lunar ventures, epics on the conquest of Istanbul and the War of Liberation, aphoristic quatrains, neomystical verse, poetry of social protest, travel impressions, books on the national liberation struggles of several countries, and humorous anecdotes in verse. Dağlarca published only poetry—more than a hundred collections in all. "In the course of a prestigious career," writes Yaşar Nabi Nayır, a prominent critic, "which started in 1934, Fazıl Hüsnü Dağlarca tried every form of poetry, achieving equally impressive success in the epic genre, in lyric and inspirational verse, in satire, and in the poetry of social criticism. Since he has contributed to Turkish literature a unique sensibility, new concepts of substance and form, and an inimitable style, his versatility and originality have been matched by few Turkish literary figures, past or present."[10] Dağlarca's tender lyric voice finds itself in countless long and short poems:

Sparkle

Clearly death is not a loss.
Regardless the brooks
Will flow.

---

10. Yaşar Nabi Nayır, "Dağlarca and His Poetry," translated by Talat S. Halman, in *Fazıl Hüsnü Dağlarca: Selected Poems* (Pittsburgh: Univ. of Pittsburgh Press, 1969), xix.

With faith
Weeds will turn green and roses will grow.
Clearly death is not a loss.

Dağlarca's protest poetry, however, can often be described as *a verbis ad verbera*.

Beating

How about it, let's join our hands.
You hit twice, and I'll belt two.
Has he stolen
Or sucked the nation's blood and sweat?
You belt four, and I'll strike four more.

Twenty sent abroad to buy ships, thirty to select tea . . .
Did the Foreign Minister get a cut,
While our hairless children starve in adobe villages,
And our baby dolls sell their pure flesh night after night?
You hit seven times, and I'll belt seven more.

How about it, eh, let's join hands.
Has he sold a plate of beans, eight cents' worth for two dollars eighty,
Or did he shake his camel's head at your petition to squeeze 500 out of
        you?
Elected to Congress did he invest in his own future, trample on progress?
You belt nine, and I'll belt nine more.

In *Toprak Ana* (Mother Earth, 1950), Dağlarca gives poetic expression to the same tragic deprivations, as in the poem "Village Without Rain":

I'm hungry, black earth, hungry, hear me.
With the black ox I'm hungry tonight.
He thinks, and thinking feeds him,
I think, and thinking makes my hunger grow.
        I'm hungry, black earth, hungry, hear me.
        One can't hide it when he's hungry.

The wind sleeps on the hills of gluttony
In the sleep of bird and beast.

Fazıl Hüsnü Dağlarca
(1914–2008)

In Turkish poetics, the quatrain holds a significant and time-honored place both as a stanzaic unit and as an independent verse. In classical poetry, its dominance was second only to the couplet, and most of the prominent poets produced—in the tradition of Omar Khayyam—an impressive body of rubais, *four-line epigrammatic verses* (a a b a). *The Turks also evolved the four-line* tuyuğ, *also in the* a a b a *rhyme pattern, but composed in a special quantitative meter and usually confined to philosophical comments. In folk poetry, the quatrain was—and still is—the essential stanzaic unit, and among its most memorable achievements are the enchorial* manis, *quatrains by anonymous poets, written in syllabic meters.*

With the advent of modernism, many structural changes, including the complete breakdown of stanzaic forms, came about. As a consequence, very few of the leading modern poets have used the quatrain. One major exception is Fazıl Hüsnü Dağlarca. In most of his multitudinous poems, Dağlarca has used the quatrain in all its aspects—rhymed and unrhymed, scanned and free, intact and fragmented.

<table>
<tr><td align="center">

Soft
The mouth
Of a hungry man
Makes the bread
Come alive

</td><td align="center">

The Faithless
When quiet
They have no tongues
When talking
They have no mouths

</td></tr>
<tr><td align="center">

Cats
The widow's
Cat
Is warmer
Than the bride's cat

</td><td align="center">

God and I
He
Is the poet of his job
I am the god
Of mine

</td></tr>
</table>

When the fat stars glide,
Darkness gets fed.
    The wind sleeps on the hills of gluttony.
    One can't sleep it off when he's hungry.

Hunger is black on our faces, hunger is hoary.
Meadows and hills hunger.
Rain falls no more and the crops are scorched.
How did we anger the skies far and wide?
    Hunger is black on our faces, hunger is hoary.
    One can't live on it when he's hungry.

Modern Turkish poetry, with its notable diversity, has arguably replicated and emulated the typology of verse in the contemporary world. It has run the gamut from rigid formality to completely free verse, from surrealism to neoclassicism, from cubism to socialist realism, from symbolism to concrete (or found) poetry. A minuscule anthology of brief excerpts and epigrammatic poems can serve as a testament to such versatility:

nebuchadnezzar turned into idols
the lovely women strolling the hanging gardens
having embraced the timeless gardens
I have kept those women to myself
                    Asaf Hâlet Çelebi (1907–58)

Let me visit you at your home,
Make me coffee;
Out of a freshly filled pitcher
Pour me water—
That's all I want
                    Ziya Osman Saba (1910–57)

Say Istanbul and towers come to mind
If I do a painting of one, the other one grumbles.
The Maiden's Tower ought to know that's the way the cookie crumbles:
She should marry the Galata Tower and have lots of kids.
                    Bedri Rahmi Eyuboğlu (1913–75)

If stars catch sight of your beauty in me
They will fall into my inmost sea one by one
And sunlight will engulf me in such splendor
You will come to me . . .

               Celâl Sılay (1914–74)

No, my lovely one,
no, my antelope-eyed,
no, my heart's conqueror.
There's one thing possible and lovely right now:
to love you up in flames.

               A. Kadir (1917–85)

So the headlines of daily papers should read:
Beam like a rose, laugh like a rose, be a rose.

               Ceyhun Atuf Kansu (1919–78)

Crows are the choicest flowers
Of my eyes

               Sabahattin Kudret Aksal (1920–93)

I know they cannot survive in the sun
Or in the aura of love
Injustice
Fear
Hunger

               Necati Cumalı (1921–2001)

All colors gathered dirt at the same speed
They gave the first prize to white.

               Özdemir Asaf (1923–81)

Does one wait for lovely days to enjoy them
Waiting itself is lovely too

               Arif Damar (b. 1925)

I had said: I want to live living,
And yet now on this roof willy-nilly

My feet and my rhymes are fettered,
My days pass with such lame feet of verse,
Don't think I'm bragging if I say so myself,
My life is the loveliest poem.

Can Yücel (1926–99)

And so on, with all those majestic rulers—
The glorious Ottoman Empire,
On whose realm the sun never set for 624 years,
Kept the whole world petrified:
It was a legend, it died.

Nüzhet Erman (1926–96)

Like a file rasping such a wind blows
Thorns glow but not the flower
The travesty of an epoch strokes its tarred surface
In its warmth blood freezes it doesn't get lukewarm
True existence straightens up on elbows
The enemy sleeps water doesn't.

Metin Eloğlu (1927–85)

The weary faces of fathers on their faces,
The mad fury of mothers on their faces;
and on their foreheads love's ineradicable seal,

—My son, my wounded father.

Özdemir İnce (b. 1936)

Glittering seas noiseless poems closing doors
Are carrying the meteors to you
The first arrow tested on the wrong target
Mumbles deliriously about you

Sezai Karakoç (b. 1933)

Drowning its passion every night in cloudy booze,
It fails to fly over the ramparts of Byzantium;
Groping through the darkness that grows dense in its heart,
It aspires to be like the poets in whose lines deer wander about.

Cevat Çapan (b. 1933)

We are the tired warriors worn down by defeat after defeat
Too timid or ashamed to enjoy a drink
Someone gathers all the suns, keeps people waiting for them
It's not the fear of shivering but warming up
We are the tired warriors, so many loves frighten us off
                    Gülten Akın (b. 1933)

"A dungeon for dreams and ideas!"
That must be
the biggest dream and idea of tyrants.
                    Ferit Edgü (b. 1936)

Every child is the clock tower of a town
in which aerialists swing toward death
the terrible tower of the death hours
one foot toward his mother the other toward death.
                    Kemal Özer (1935–2009)

Poetry is fire's messenger,
the arsonist.
It is the bird perched on the volcano.
                    Ülkü Tamer (b. 1937)

Poet you too took the path of your ancestors
I fear your weight cannot carry those countless calamities
                    Cahit Zarifoğlu (1940–87)

Only the tears of others
will remain from this love
and as you know it is always others who are witness
to death and life
                    Melisa Gürpınar (b. 1941)

Suffering is the slow horse that trots back the distance it rode
Life's hidden and ill-omened birdlime.
It makes us taste unexpected joys
And lends color to a bird's wings,

Ripping the night open, weaving the day
It shows what simply doesn't exist as existing.

Metin Altıok (1941–93)

My homeland is dragging me down and now I am like a house
whose plaster has fallen off
It's about to collapse, useless, ugly
Love me, guard the warmth of the kiss where your hair comes together
Prepare your hands to stay in my palms for years on end.

Ataol Behramoğlu (b. 1942)

What we craft is a great song. Each melody has lasted
    a hundred years. Its end is a tale. What we
    graft is a great song if only it could last
    long after us . . .

Sennur Sezer (b. 1943)

White angels swim through its waters
human destiny, a scattered torso
now the world's suns and the moon's daybreak winds are growing pale
wilting at the soaring grove
and the moon glides with its silver rowboat into the roots of trees

Gülseli İnal (b. 1947)

the swans too are bound to darken
if death is narration
some days our bourgeoise necks will lose
their passion for stout ropes anyway

Murathan Mungan (b. 1955)

no one catches sight
of the wild ducks in the deltas
or the way they fall off the backs
of the female ducks

no one knows
but no one!

that those red ants
piercing right through the sand hills
are lovers in great suffering

Adnan Özer (b. 1957)

The abundance of poetry in the Turkish Republic is such that it is virtually impossible to do justice to it in a concise history. Well into its ninth decade, the republic had witnessed the publication of tens of thousands of poems in periodicals and many thousands of poetry books by hundreds of poets. Even major anthologies often fail to deal judiciously with the full range of the country's enormous poetic output. In the present brief history, one can only regret the omission of innumerable names, among them such masters of syllabic meters as Ahmet Kutsi Tecer, Orhan Seyfi Orhon, Ömer Bedrettin Uşaklı, Mustafa Seyit Sutüven, Halit Fahri Ozansoy, Ümit Yaşar Oğuzcan; neoclassicists such as Mehmet Çınarlı, Bekir Sıtkı Erdoğan, and Faruk Nafiz Çamlıbel (a virtuoso equally adept at *aruz* prosody and syllabic meters); Behçet Kemal Çağlar, an exuberant patriotic poet; and effective users of free verse such as Orhon Murat Arıburnu, Cengiz Bektaş, Ahmet Necdet, Ebubekir Eroğlu, Şükran Kurdakul, Güven Turan, Tahsin Saraç, Refik Durbaş, Küçük İskender, Lâle Müldür, Ali Püsküllüoğlu, Turgay Gönenç, Ahmet Erhan, Tarık Günersel, and scores of others. Such richness certainly makes poetry aficionados happy but frustrates anthologists and literary historians.

The early novels of the republic depicted the disintegration of Ottoman society, ferocious political enmities, and the immoral lives of some members of religious sects, as well as the conflicts between urban intellectuals and poverty-stricken peasants—as in the novels of Yakup Kadri Karaosmanoğlu (1889–1974). Turkey's major female intellectual and advocate of women's rights, Halide Edib Adıvar (1882–1964), produced sagas of the War of Liberation, psychological novels, and panoramas of city life. Her novelistic art culminated in *Sinekli Bakkal* (1936), which she originally published in English in 1935 under the title *The Clown and His Daughter*.

The harsh realities of Anatolia found fertile ground in the literature of engagement after World War II. Sabahattin Ali (1907–48) was a pioneer of forceful fiction about the trials and tribulations of the lower classes. Two books, both published in 1950—*Bizim Köy* (Our Village; *A Village in Anatolia*) by Mahmut Makal (b. 1930) and *Toprak Ana* by Fazıl Hüsnü

Dağlarca—exerted a shattering impact on political and intellectual circles by dramatically exposing conditions in villages. The first, available in English translation, is a series of vignettes written by Makal, a teenage peasant who became a village teacher after graduating from one of the controversial Institutes for Village Teachers. The book reveals the abject poverty of the Anatolian village:

> Quite apart from the trouble of earning the wretched stuff, it's difficult even to make bread here in any edible form. . . . The women rise at night, knead the dough, and while their husbands are still in bed—that is to say, before dawn—they bake enough for the day. If they get up a bit late, they get no end of a beating from their husbands, and everyone calls them "slatterns." . . . If you want to know what the torments of Hell are like, I'd say it's baking bread in this village.
>
> Not five per cent of the women in our village wear shoes. All the rest go barefoot. Even in winter they do the same, in the snow and the mud and the wet. The girls all go barefoot. . . . And in summer these same feet go off to the cornfields to plough, all cracked and cut with stones.[11]

In the mid-1950s, a brave new genre emerged—the "Village Novel," which reached its apogee with Yaşar Kemal's *İnce Memed* (translated into English under the title *Memed, My Hawk,* 1961). Yaşar Kemal (b. 1923), the most famous twentieth-century Turkish novelist at home and abroad, was frequently mentioned not only in Turkey but also in the world press and literary circles as a strong candidate for the Nobel Prize. His impressive corpus of fiction, written in a virtually poetic style, ranks as one of the truly stirring achievements in the history of Turkish literature.

Dealing with the merciless reality of poverty, village literature portrays the peasant threatened by natural disaster and man's inhumanity. The drama is enacted in terms of economic and psychological deprivation, blood feuds, stagnation and starvation, droughts, the tyranny of the gendarmes and petty officials, and exploitation at the hands of landowners and politicos. The lithe style records local dialects with an almost flawless accuracy. A pessimistic tone pervades much of village literature: its

11. Mahmut Makal, *A Village in Anatolia,* translated by Sir Wyndham Deedes (London: Vallentine, Mitchell, 1954), 22–23, 61.

delineations are bleak even when occasional flashes of humor or a glimmer of hope or descriptions of nature's beauty appear. A great strength of the genre is its freedom from the rhetoric that mars much of the poetry of social protest. When presenting deprived men and women pitted against hostile forces, the best practitioners offered an affirmation of the human spirit. Their works are often testaments to the dauntless determination of the peasant to survive and to resist—sometimes through rebellion—the forces of oppression.

Urban writers deal with a broad diversity of social problems in major cities. Accomplished novelist Abdülhak Şinasi Hisar (1888–1963) enjoys fame for nostalgic and sometimes satiric depictions of high-class life in old Istanbul. Peyami Safa (1899–1961), one of Turkey's most prolific authors, deals with social problems, cultural tensions, and psychic crises in his many highly readable novels.

Fiction about the urban poor shares some of the strengths of the Village Novel—engrossing plot, effective narration, realistic dialogue—and suffers from some of the comparable flaws—lack of subtlety and of psychological depth. The leading writer of fiction depicting the tribulations of working-class people is Orhan Kemal (1914–70). Necati Cumalı (1921–2001), a prolific poet and playwright, wrote tellingly about poverty-sticken individuals in rural and coastal areas. Osman Cemal Kaygılı (1890–1945) penned poignant stories of the lumpenproletariat and the gypsies.

The short-story writer Sait Faik (1906–54) is admired for his meditative, rambling romantic fiction, full of intriguing insights into the human soul, capturing the pathos and the bathos of urban life in a style unique for its poetic yet colloquial flair.

Sait Faik's career, which spanned barely twenty-five years from about 1929 to 1954, yielded an output that displays a considerable variety of themes and techniques although virtually all of his stories have certain similarities—his unmistakable style, the focal importance of the narrator, the preoccupation with social outcasts and marginal groups, and an unfaltering ear for colloquial speech. His stories can in their range of feeling and creative strategies be likened to many disparate works by some of his predecessors, contemporaries, and successors outside Turkey. One occasionally finds plots worthy of a de Maupassant, moods reminiscent of a Chekhov, and sometimes the lucidity of a Maugham, although none of these writers—not even some of the French writers Sait Faik presumably read during his stay in Grenoble—seems to have had any direct influence on him. In some stories, the Turkish writer gives us a blend of fantasy and concrete fact as well as the interplay of different levels of reality in the Faulknerian manner. In others, one finds a structural clarity and a crispness of language typical of Hemingway. Sait Faik's later stories occasionally read like Donald Barthelme's early work, sharing the same eerie sensations of a foray into the realms of fantasy.

Cevat Şakir (1886–1973), who adopted the pen name "Halikarnas Balıkçısı" (The Fisherman of Halicarnassus), a polyglot who also wrote in English, produced gripping novels about common people, especially fishermen, on the Aegean coast.

An awakening of interest in Ottoman history after several decades of neglect gave rise to a massive semidocumentary novel by Kemal Tahir (1910–73), *Devlet Ana* (Mother State, 1967), a saga of the emergence of the Ottoman state in the late thirteenth and early fourteenth centuries. The Turkish War of Liberation (1919–22), as in the previous decades, inspired numerous major novels—*Yorgun Savaşçı* (The Tired Warrior, 1965) by Kemal Tahir, *Kalpaklılar* (Men in Fur Caps, 1962) and *Doludizgin* (Full Gallop, 1963) by Samim Kocagöz (1916–93), and *Kutsal İsyan* (The Sacred Uprising, 1966–68), in eight volumes, by Hasan İzzettin Dinamo (1909–89).

Attilâ İlhan produced a two-volume portrayal (à la Dos Passos's *U.S.A.*) of the crises of Turkish society following World War II, entitled *Kurtlar Sofrası* (A Feast for Wolves, 1963).

The best social realists in the second half of the twentieth century include Fakir Baykurt (1929–99), Çetin Altan (b. 1927), Dursun Akçam (1930–2003), Talip Apaydın (b. 1926), Tarık Dursun K. (b. 1931), Vedat Türkali (b. 1919), Kemal Bilbaşar (1910–83), Mehmet Seyda (1919–86), and Zeyyat Selimoğlu (1922–2000). Highly imaginative fiction came from Nahit Sırrı Örik (1894–1960), who wrote compellingly about the late Ottoman period, as did Hıfzı Topuz (b. 1923), a writer of semidocumentary fiction. Another major figure is Peride Celal (b. 1916), whose work evolved from popular novels to sophisticated psychological fiction and an epic treatment of democracy beset by conflicts. Sevim Burak (1931–83) was a successful practitioner of Faulknerian narrative techniques. A multi-talented author, Zülfü Livaneli (b. 1946) has to his credit many diverse novels, some of which have enjoyed considerable success in Turkey, as have their translations abroad. The short-story scene, which was dominated in the mid–twentieth century by such figures as Sait Faik, Memduh Şevket Esendal (1883–1952), and Nezihe Meriç (1925–2009) and later by Tomris Uyar (1941–2003) and Sevgi Soysal (1936–76), now flourishes thanks to the work of Cemil Kavukçu (b. 1951), Hasan Ali Toptaş (b. 1958), and others.

In the closing decades of the twentieth century, Turkish fiction enjoyed a remarkable growth in maturity and expanded its typology. Its development and diversity are difficult to trace in such a condensed history. All that can be done in such a study is to cite the names of the most successful fiction writers and to pay lip service to some of the movements, titles, and characteristics. The major writers who emerged in the late 1960s include Leylâ Erbil (b. 1931), an imaginative storyteller; Oğuz Atay (1934–77), who made a very strong impact with his *Tutunamayanlar* (The Maladjusted, 1971–72); Yusuf Atılgan, a maverick writer about psychological misfits; İhsan Oktay Anar, who brought stimulating dimensions to historical episodes; Ayşe Kulin, who is the author of several exciting best-sellers, some based on the life experiences of her family members; Tahsin Yücel, one of the most accomplished and versatile novelists ever to write in the Turkish language; Feyyaz Kayacan, who has crafted engrossing nightmarish stories of World War II; Abbas Sayar, who wrote a *succès d'estime* about an old horse; Osman Necmi Gürmen, who has produced notable novels about modern Turkish society and Ottoman events; Gülten Dayıoğlu and Mustafa Ruhi Şirin, two of the many accomplished writers of children's fiction; Öner Yağcı, who has effectively depicted the aftermath of a military coup; Feride Çiçekoğlu, who is well known for fanciful fiction; and Demir Özlü and Burhan Günel, who enjoy a loyal following for their craftsmanlike narratives. Nedim Gürsel's novels about Ottoman history and modern Turkey win hosannas not only in his homeland, but also in Europe and elsewhere.

Among contemporary masters of fiction are such highly successful authors as Ayla Kutlu, İnci Aral, Erendiz Atasü, Pınar Kür, Alev Alatlı. The field of fiction is often dominated by powerful novels that come from Murathan Mungan, Selim İleri, Mehmet Eroğlu, and Ahmet Altan.

Turkish-style magical realism is quite strong thanks to the remarkable novels of Latife Tekin, Nazlı Eray, Buket Uzuner, and Aslı Erdoğan, whose works have been translated into several major languages, especially English.

Satirical fiction is still dominated by Aziz Nesin (1916–95), Turkey's best satirist ever. In scores of books, Nesin strongly indicts the oppression and brutalization of the common man. His hero is the man in the street beleaguered by the inimical forces of modern life. He lambastes bureaucracy and exposes economic inequities in stories that effectively combine local color and universal verities.

Seldom in the course of Turkish literature has there been a gentler and more effective satirist of hypocrisy, sham, and a whole range of foibles than Haldun Taner (1915–86), who always wrote with empathy and compassion and out of a powerful faith in the perfectibility of the human being. Interestingly, Nesin, Turkey's supreme satirist, who was born a year later than Taner, held very little optimism that the human personality will improve but believed that a new ideological structuring might redeem society.

In sharp contrast to realist fiction, a group of authors, some well versed in English and French, produced stream-of-consciousness fiction heavily influenced by Joyce and Faulkner as well as by the French *nouveau roman*. Their works depict psychological crises in lyrical and sometimes turgid styles. Some of them offer tragicomic scenes of modern life by means of a decomposed language. The principal themes of modern fiction all over the world also characterize the Turkish *nouvelle vague:* dehumanization, moral disintegration, absurdity, lack of heroism, ennui, futility, hypocrisy. The protagonists are often abstractions of psychic turmoil, and phenomena are presented in terms of transmogrification. The leading authors of this mode of fiction—Feyyaz Kayacan (1919–93), Bilge Karasu (1930–95), Orhan Duru (1933–2009)—expanded the scope of psychic experiences in Turkish literature and, while forcing the language to the breaking point, enriched expressive resources and rhythmic formulations.

Oktay Akbal (b. 1923) shares with this group a Kafkaesque sense of reality and utter despair although he departs from them in his use of a simple staccato—almost pointillistic—style. But both the *nouveau roman* writers and Akbal chart the phantasmagoria of man's tormented soul and his alienation from nature and society.

Since the 1980s, the art of the novel has taken giant strides in Turkey thanks in part to the growing corpus of Yaşar Kemal and to the impressive work of Adalet Ağaoğlu (b. 1929), Tahsin Yücel (b. 1933), Vüs'at O. Bener (1922–2005), Erhan Bener (1929–2007), Attilâ İlhan, and others. Elif Şafak (b. 1971) enjoys wide fame internationally thanks to her provocative novels that interfuse traditional values and innovative features. The first decade of the twenty-first century has enjoyed what can be characterized as "the post-postmodern" fiction of numerous younger writers—for instance, Tuna Kiremitçi, Müge İplikçi, Perihan Mağden, Cezmi Ersöz, Şebnem İyigüzel, and Sema Kaygusuz, as well as Ahmet Ümit (b. 1960), who is gaining wide recognition as a master of suspense thrillers, a rare genre in Turkey.

In Turkey and abroad, Orhan Pamuk (b. 1952) has emerged as a compelling precursor of new dimensions in the Turkish novelistic art. His major works have been successfully translated into nearly fifty languages, the English versions attracting wide attention and winning a number of major international awards. Pamuk's meteoric rise culminated in his winning the Nobel Prize for Literature in 2006. It is significant that this first Nobel Prize won by a Turk in any field went to a literary figure because literature remains the premier cultural genre among Turks. Pamuk himself asserted that the prize was awarded principally to Turkish language and literature. Although some intellectuals acknowledge this to be a fact, many believe that the prize was awarded in recognition of Pamuk's own creative work; some claim he received the prize because he made damaging remarks about incidents in Ottoman history and contemporary life. Pamuk's formula for success has been postmodernism plus some Turkish exoticism. He has been likened to several giants of modern literature. Such kinships tend to provide a fairly easy passage to fame abroad. The risk involved, however, is that similarities may not sustain the inherent value of the oeuvre for long—unless the writer from the other culture finds a voice uniquely his own, explores new forms, and creates a synthesis beyond a pat formula based on what is in fashion.

Critics enamored of identifying models and influences have discovered affinities between Pamuk and Borges, Calvino, and Eco, whose works he has probably devoured. A voracious reader, he has stated that, "especially from age sixteen to twenty-five, I read like mad and aspired to resemble the authors I admired most." On another occasion, he observed: "If we must use Western criteria, for me the novel of the Western world is the creative work of Joyce, Proust, Woolf, Faulkner, and Nabokov—not Hemingway and Steinbeck, who have long been idolized in our country for their simplicity of style and language."

It would not be incorrect, however, to assert that Pamuk is at present proceeding away from "influences" toward an authentic, original novelistic art—a new synthesis as evinced by his post-Nobel novel, *Masumiyet Müzesi* (2008; *The Museum of Innocence,* 2009). His first novel, *Cevdet Bey ve Oğulları* (Cevdet Bey and His Sons, 1982) is a Buddenbrooks type of work in three volumes that traces a family's life over three generations as well as the process of Turkish modernization from the early twentieth century onward. *Sessiz Ev* (Quiet House, 1983) skillfully fuses modern and traditional novelistic techniques, utilizing five major characters who narrate the story through their stream of consciousness. The latter two works remain untranslated into English, although both have fascinating features. *Beyaz Kale* (1985), published in English translation in 1990 as *The White Castle,* is a tour de force about the intriguing interaction between a Venetian and an Ottoman look-alike who symbolize diverse aspects of the cultural tensions between East and West.

Kara Kitap (1990; *The Black Book,* 1994 and 2006) was hailed as a masterwork, especially in Europe and the United States, and solidified Pamuk's reputation. It masterfully depicts the mysteries of Istanbul and evokes the traditional values of Sufism. *Yeni Hayat* (1995; *The New Life,* 1997) is a travel novel woven in a poetic style that deals with imagination gone awry, youthful despair, and republican idealism thwarted.

The success of two novels in particular—*Benim Adım Kırmızı* (1998; *My Name Is Red,* 2001), a powerful novel about miniature painters in the Ottoman capital in 1591, and *Kar* (2002; *Snow,* 2004), Pamuk's most patently political work—led to his Nobel Prize. His *İstanbul: Hatıralar ve Şehir* (2003; *Istanbul: Memories and the City,* 2005), a beguilingly evocative description of his beloved and sorrowful city, enhanced his international prestige. His *Masumiyet Müzesi* is avowedly a novel of love, marriage, friendship, sexuality, family life, and happiness. Pamuk was crowned the novel's success by opening a museum by the same name in Istanbul.

A most remarkable development in the Turkish arts has been the explosion of theatrical activity and the strides made in dramatic writing. Very few cities in the world have a broader spectrum of plays or superior performances presented than Istanbul. In 1960, Istanbul audiences had a choice of fewer than ten plays on any given day, but of more than thirty by the end of the decade; the increase in Ankara in the same period was from five to about twenty. In the second half of the twentieth century, an amazing diversity of foreign plays was produced, including *Hamlet* (four separate productions), *My Fair Lady, Marat / Sade, South Pacific, Antigone,*

French vaudevilles, *The Caretaker, The Odd Couple, Tobacco Road, The Diary of a Madman, Mother Courage, The Miser, Who's Afraid of Virginia Woolf, Fiddler on the Roof, The Physicists,* and *Oh Dad, Poor Dad.* The Turkish theater fared well not only in terms of quantity, but also in terms of the quality of production and performance: many observers, comparing Turkish versions to their European, British, and American originals or counterparts, testified that Turkish theaters often did just as well and sometimes better.

The spectrum of dramatic literature by Turkish playwrights is now impressively broad: from well-made family melodramas to Brechtian works such as Sermet Çağan's *Ayak Bacak Fabrikası* (The Orthopedic Factory) and Haldun Taner's *Keşanlı Ali Destanı* (*The Ballad of Ali of Keshan,* 1970);[12] from light comedies to Güngör Dilmen's scathing drama of innocent people brutalized by capitalism and imperialism; from striking village plays by Cahit Atay and Necati Cumalı to an Albee-like black comedy by Melih Cevdet Anday; from Aziz Nesin's modernized version of *Karagöz,* the traditional shadow play, to Refik Erduran's Shakespearean tragedy about Justinian the Great; from a musical drama by Turgut Özakman and Bülent Arel depicting city youth to A. Turan Oflazoğlu's towering tragedy in verse about the Ottoman sultan İbrahim "the Mad"; from Orhan Kemal's prison drama to Orhan Asena's dramatizations of history and legends.

A remarkable talent emerged in the closing decades of the twentieth century—Memet Baydur (1951–2001) brought new visions and vitality to playwriting with imaginative innovations. His premature death deprived the Turkish theater of stimulating works that might have found their way into many theatrical capitals abroad as well.

The foremost pioneer of the study of the history of modern Turkish theater, Metin And, devised an encompassing typology in his books *A History of Theatre and Popular Entertainment in Turkey* and *50 Yılın Türk Tiyatrosu* (The Turkish Theater of the Past Fifty Years): plays about idealistic heroes, social reformers, political leaders battling against corruption, political tyranny, and social injustice; plays depending largely on character portrayal; plays on dreams, memory, and psychoanalytical themes; plays depicting women's and artists' problems; plays about the eternal triangle

12. The play was first produced in 1967.

and marital problems in general; plays on social injustice, bureaucracy, urban-rural conflicts; detective plays, murder mysteries, suspense thrillers; family dramas, including those about the generation gap; verse melodramas; village dramas and plays about life in shantytowns; plays about the previous civilizations of Anatolia; plays about the maladjusted; dramas dealing with abstract concepts and hypothetical situations; light comedies and vaudevilles; satires of traditional values and current life; the play-within-a-play; modernizations of shadow plays and *commedia dell'arte;* plotless plays; dramas based on folk legends and Turkish history; expressionistic plays; sentimental dramas; epic theater; cabaret theater; plays based on Greek tragedy; theater of the absurd and musical drama.[13]

Another major scholar-critic, Sevda Şener, has observed the following about aspects of Turkish playwriting:

> The most conspicuous achievement of contemporary Turkish dramatic writing and production has been the conscious effort to create original native drama by making use of the formal and stylistic elements of traditional spectacular plays in a way to satisfy modern taste and contemporary intellectual needs. The main challenge to such an attempt is to preserve critical sensitivity and to discriminate between the easy attraction of the spectacular and the pleasure of witnessing the true combination of form and content.[14]

From the middle of the twentieth century on, according to Dikmen Gürün, a notable theater critic, "the [Turkish] playwrights' quest was focused on the issues of rural migration, feudal social order and life in the slums. . . . [T]he system was questioned in all its aspects. In later years, influenced by the current political theater in Europe, the Turkish playwrights began to deal with the issue in a similar form and content. They employed the episodic form of epic and merged it with the traditional Turkish norms."[15]

---

13. Metin And, *A History of Theatre and Popular Entertainment* (Ankara: Forum, 1963–64), 102–10, and *50 Yılın Türk Tiyatrosu* (Istanbul: Türkiye İş Bankası, 1973), 490–637.

14. Sevda Şener, "Turkish Drama," available at http://sanat.bilkent.edu.tr/interactive .m2.org/Theater/SSener.html.

15. Dikmen Gürün, "An Excursion in the Turkish Theater," available at http://sanat .bilkent.edu.tr/interactive/m2.org/Theater/dikmen.html.

Theater in Turkey, all its shortcomings and weaknesses aside, can still legitimately boast of remarkable achievements that have enabled it to move far ahead of theater not only in all developing countries, but also in many advanced countries that have a longer theatrical tradition and substantially greater resources. The record of Turkish dramatic arts is, by any objective criterion, impressive.

The second half of the twentieth century witnessed strides taken in literary criticism when Nurullah Ataç (1898–1957) achieved renown as an impressionistic critic who reevaluated the tradition of classical poetry and spearheaded the values inherent in ventures of new poetry, especially "The First New" movement. An exciting and enduring contribution came from Ahmet Hamdi Tanpınar, a prominent Turkish litterateur and an eloquent exponent of a generation of intellectuals who made a synthesis of classical Turkish culture, French literature, and modern artistic sensibilities. A first-rate poet and novelist as well as an inspiring professor of literature at Istanbul University, he wrote a monumental critical history of Turkish literature, *Ondokuzuncu Asır Türk Edebiyatı Tarihi* (History of Nineteenth-Century Turkish Literature, 1949), and a superb treatise on the famous neoclassical poet Yahya Kemal, published in 1962.

Among academic critics, Orhan Burian (1914–53) held the promise of a strong impact on the evaluation of modern Turkish poetry, but his life was cut short by his premature death.

Mehmet Kaplan (1915–86) made astute analyses of poetry and short fiction of the period from the nineteenth century onward. He also produced numerous stimulating studies of early Turkish literature. One flaw in his work resulted from various lapses of judgment regarding many of his contemporaries, especially Nazım Hikmet and other socialist writers.

The vast amount of socialist literary criticism proved ideologically effective in the second half of the twentieth century. Cevdet Kudret (1907–92), Memet Fuat (1926–2002), Selahattin Hilav (1928–2005), Asım Bezirci (1927–93), Fethi Naci (1927–2008), and others were the notable members of this school. Sabahattin Eyuboğlu (1908–73), Vedat Günyol (1911–2004), Adnan Benk (1922–98), and Murat Belge (b. 1943) excelled in producing urbane and erudite essays. Ideologically impartial critical work came from Suut Kemal Yetkin (1903–80), Azra Erhat (1915–82), Hüseyin Cöntürk (1918–2003), Tahir Alangu (1916–73), Rauf Mutluay (1925–95), Konur Ertop (b. 1936), and others.

The most prolific reviewer of all time, Doğan Hızlan (b. 1937), functions as the "conscience" of Turkish literature, setting the lead among fair-minded and stimulating critics. This group also includes Ahmet Oktay (b. 1933), Adnan Binyazar (b. 1934), Adnan Özyalçıner (b. 1934), Orhan Koçak (b. 1948), Feridun Andaç (b. 1954), Semih Gümüş (b. 1956), Füsun Akatlı (1944–2010), Cem Erciyes, Ömer Türkeş, Cemil Meriç (1916–87), Nermi Uygur (1925–2005), Beşir Ayvazoğlu (b. 1952), Hasan Bülent Kahraman, and others.

Berna Moran (1921–93), a scholar of English literature, produced several major books about literary theories and their applicability to Turkish literature that have become guidebooks for critics in the succeeding decades. Jale Parla (b. 1945), who earned a doctorate in comparative literature at Harvard University, stands as perhaps the most important Turkish academic critic of fiction, especially on the strength of her major work *Don Kişot'tan Bugüne Roman* (The Novel from Don Quixote to Our Day).

Dilek Doltaş (b. 1945), Yıldız Ecevit (b. 1946), Sibel Irzık (b. 1958), Nurdan Gürbilek (b. 1956), and Nüket Esen (b. 1949) are among accomplished academic critics.

Enis Batur (b. 1952), who also enjoys fame as a poet and publisher, possesses one of the most interesting literary minds of his generation and in many respects stands as the ideal symbol of and spokesman for the cultural synthesis that modern Turkey has been striving to create.

A salutary observation about literary criticism is that it has never been more evenhanded or objective, never as free from ideological bias or polemics. It benefits from Turkey's widest freedom heretofore for writers. It is probably more refined than ever and will most likely take impressive strides if its practitioners rely less on the literary theories that abound in the Western world and create some of its own that will serve more effectively in evaluating the sui generis identity and authentic aesthetic values.

The past millennium of Turkish literature can justifiably be characterized as many-splendored. Its oral tradition in verse and narration as well as its written legacy in all genres stand as testaments to the nation's imagination and creativity. In a thousand years, it stretched from Central

Beacon

Jutting far into the high seas, the promontory,
Cherished as the lazulite and silver night, smolders.
A terrestrial love starts in the dark
While the beacon shines
Despite destiny on the boulders.

Clouds fuse in crepuscular dimensions,
From distant harbors fogs descend,
And sadness stirs in the darkness of fate;
Blazing and blinking, the beacon inquires:
Where in life do you stand, where in love do you stand?

If the heart cringes in the starlight,
Memories might recede and recoil.
Time may tread on without the soul's cargo
As the beacon has stood for ages
With patience on this same soil.

It witnessed sea battles and ancient pirates,
Caught the wind asleep and the waves in flight,
As blue and black as a single eye,
And vacant as the vast seas;
Ill-fated fishermen struggled in its sight.

In your hair a cool air smells of salt and death.
On your face a cyclone's tastes linger.
You stand weary and forlorn,
Suddenly flickering, quivering with joy:
Something, perhaps life, is now longer.

Dolorous as the widows' indomitable desires,
Upon its prowess the gargantuan night lies.
Insane, taciturn, and awake,
It craves from disaster the charity of end-all;
It is wise.

Our drunken vessels roll and sway.
The sleep of buried hurricanes is stirred,
Rocks stretch far like pelagic graves,
From the sea to heaven
The sailor's curse is heard.

Time vanishes and life abandons time;
From the galaxies descend no bulletins.
Heavy and tired with an ill omen,
When all men are thought to have ceased,
The beacon grins.

Fazıl Hüsnü Dağlarca (1914–2008)

Asia to the Caucasus, the Middle East, the Balkans, and points beyond. It embraced influences from the East and the West, the North and the South. As a consequence, it created its own synthesis, which came to include the aesthetic strategies of Europe and the Americas. Its explorations and diversity of accomplishments are admirable. Its universal work was "certified" when the Nobel Prize for Literature was awarded to the novelist Orhan Pamuk in 2006.

The second millennium of this time-honored and vigorous literature will probably be marked by countless impressive achievements.

AFTERWORD
The Future of Turkish Literature

IT IS A TRUISM that poetry dominated Turkish literature for nearly a thousand years. In the latter part of the twentieth century, though, poetry was eclipsed by fiction, which established its hegemony in the present age.

Orhan Pamuk's winning the Nobel Prize for Literature in 2006 certainly played a major role in this phenomenon, although it would not be incorrect to assert that the novel genre might have become ascendant even without Pamuk's singular achievement.

Prior to the inroads that Europeanization made into Turkish culture around the mid–nineteenth century, elite poets (and intellectuals in general) had spurned prose as being easy, as inferior to verse. By the same token, oral folk poetry had held sway in the rural areas, and it could also rightfully boast of fascinating creativity in tales and narratives.

Now, in the early twenty-first century, Turkish verse seems to be suffering from tired blood. Gone are the paragons and legendary masters. In the past, many of those luminaries stood as acclaimed cultural heroes. Today, the few revered figures are in their eighties or nineties. Although some younger practitioners have managed to gain recognition, many of the poetic talents that emerged in the 1980s have since channeled their creative energies into fiction. Numerous major publishers have been forced to terminate or suspend the publication of poetry books and anthologies. Sales of such books are now paltry. The reading public, once enamored of poetry in books and magazines, seems to have abandoned its passion. In this sense, Turkey is experiencing the decline that played havoc with the popularity and prestige of poetry in the English-speaking world, Europe, and Latin America several decades earlier.

Not that the current poetic output is of a lesser caliber. Simply put, poetic creativity is overshadowed by the novel's current power. What compounds the problem is that most of the successful Turkish verses are abstruse, obscurantist, and inaccessible—too demanding at a time when the public revels in the Internet's easy appeal.

A similar downtrend is observed in dramatic writing when it is compared with the plays that achieved impressive success in the latter part of the twentieth century. Even those major playwrights of that period who are still alive have stopped writing plays, or they appear to have become less virtuosic. New talents that might have been expected to write for the theater are concentrating on more lucrative television series or films. There looms the peril of the live stage giving way to the screen. Yet the theaters (run by the state, major or small municipalities, independents, and universities) continue to stimulate extensive theatrical activity. Although the current scene is dominated by revivals, non-Turkish classics, and translations of modern European and American hits, its vitality is such that high-quality native playwriting is bound to have a resurgence.

Literary criticism seems likely to enjoy its golden age in the coming decades. Creative writing had for a millennium produced a huge corpus, including masterworks in many genres, without the benefit of critical guidance. Scholarship and literary history, too, had lagged, notwithstanding some rare exceptions. The essay form has become extraordinarily successful since the late nineteenth century, however, and holds the promise of remaining so in the foreseeable future.

Turkish criticism now seems to be on the eve of estimable achievements. With great élan, scholars, academic critics, and professional reviewers are beginning to produce refined evaluations of modern works as well as of Turkey's long literary heritage. This output will probably include excellent histories of Turkish culture and literature.

Novels and short stories in Turkey can be ranked as world class. The modernist Yaşar Kemal, a Nobel Prize contender for decades, is esteemed as a master of fiction. And Nobel laureate Orhan Pamuk, a postmodernist par excellence, continues to enjoy international popularity.

The diversity of creativity in the genre of fiction in Turkey is astounding, as is the virtuosity. From stark realism to stream of consciousness, from historical adventure to magical realism, from psychological suspense to sweeping sagas, Turkish authors have squeezed into half a century virtually the entire experience of European, American, and Latin American fiction. Their achievement is remarkable because although emulating that monumental legacy, they have also been able to avoid imitation and to endow their works with an authentic Turkish personality.

In the early part of the third millennium, the literature of the Turkish Republic can justifiably boast of a prodigious creative energy and some impressive success in many genres. It has yet to reach the threshold of greatness. It is faced with some impediments: *cultural convulsion* (cataclysmic changes in sociopolitical institutions, faith, and technology); *language crisis* (a vast transformation, broader than the language reform undertaken by any other nation, in which a vocabulary that consisted of 75 percent Arabic, Persian, and French words in 1920 increased its ratio of native words to 80 percent and reduced borrowings to only 20 percent by 1970, and the language functioning at the turn of the twenty-first century has about one hundred thousand dictionary entries); *critical gap* (despite some fine critical writing, Turkish literature still operates by and large without the guidance of coherent aesthetic theories and systematic critical analysis); *traditional lacunae* (the noticeable absence of philosophy, of the norms of tragedy, of psychological analysis in depth); and *excessive imitation* of models, movements, and major works that have evolved in the West.

The dynamism, quality, purpose, diversity, and impact of modern Turkish literature seem impressive. There is a fertile versatility at work. Turkish literature has never been more varied or more inclusive. Following many decades of conscious experimentation, questing for new values, acquisition of deeper literary and human insights, and stronger expertise in blending form and content, Turkish authors are creating an authentic synthesis of national and universal elements.

In the early phase of its second millennium, Turkish literature stands as both old and new, mature and youthful. It is a unique synthesis nurtured by a nation's vivid imagination. It confidently looks forward to its future as a powerful force in world literature.

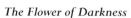

The Flower of Darkness

I set foot on the soil of this world
as if I was making love to a sleeping woman
The hot bees of my eyes kept landing
on the bushes of silence and flying off again
All for nothing their feet were covered with flowerdust

I am unrelenting pain the trees are deaf
Dawn's distilled steel is no comfort for me
All for nothing day arrives its lances
cannot hoodwink me I have read
the fable of land and sea
the simple tale of birth and death

I found the Flower of Darkness in the forest
like the blindman's armband with three dots
The sea's desolate banner is all for nothing
The bird that carries the vision to its nest
The moon's padlock over the sky all for nothing

Melih Cevdet Anday (1915–2002)

SUGGESTED READING

INDEX

BIOGRAPHICAL NOTES

SUGGESTED READING

The list given here contains books in English relating to Turkish literature (translations, anthologies, histories, critical studies) published in North America, England, Turkey, and elsewhere from 1850 on. It is not a complete or exhaustive list: numerous titles not available in libraries or for sale have not been included. (No works by Mevlana Celaleddin Rumi, who wrote his entire corpus in Persian, are included in this list.)

The list demonstrates that whereas about twenty titles were published in English from 1850 to 1950, the first decade of the twenty-first century has seen the publication of more than one hundred titles.

1850   *Turkish Evening Entertainments: The Wonders of Remarkable Incidents,* John P. Brown, trans. (New York: Putnam).

1854   *Pleasing Tales of Khoja Nasr-iddeen Efendi,* William Burchardt Bater (London).

1884   *The Turkish Jester; or, the Pleasantries of Cogia Nasr Eddin Efendi,* George Barrow, trans. (Ipswich, U.K.: W. Webber).

1898   *Told in the Coffee House,* Cyrus Adler and Allan Ramsay (New York: Macmillan).

1900–1909   *A History of Ottoman Poetry,* 6 vols., E. J. W. Gibb (London: Luzac; reprint, Cambridge, U.K.: Trustees of the "E. J. W. Gibb Memorial," 1963–84).

1901   *Ottoman Literature: The Poets and Poetry of Turkey,* E. J. W. Gibb (London: M. W. Dunne).

1901   *Turkish Fairy Tales and Folk Tales,* Ignácz Kúnos, comp. (London: A. H. Bullen).

1901   *Turkish Literature: Comprising Fables, Belles-Lettres, and Sacred Traditions,* Epiphanius Wilson, trans. (London: Colonial).

1913   *Forty-Four Turkish Fairy Tales,* Ignácz Kúnos (London: Harrap).

1916   *The Pleasantries of Cogia Nasr Eddin Effendi,* George Borrow, trans. (Cleveland, Ohio: Clerk's).

1923	*The Khoja: Tales of Nasr-ed-din*, Henry Dudley Barnham, trans. (London: Nisbet).
1924	*The Shirt of Flame*, Halide Edib Adıvar (New York: Duffield).
1926	*Memoirs of Halide Edip*, Halide Edib Adıvar (New York: Century); reprinted as *House with Wisteria: Memoirs of Halide Edib* with an introduction by Sibel Erol (Charlottesville, Va.: Leopolis, 2003).
1933	*The Turkish Theatre*, Nicholas N. Martinovitch (New York: Theatre Arts).
1935	*The Clown and His Daughter*, Halide Edib Adıvar (London: Allen and Unwin).
1943	*The Mevlid-i Sherif*, Süleyman Çelebi; F. Lyman MacCallum, trans. (London: J. Murray).
1943	*Once the Hodja*, Alice Geer Kelsey (New York: Longmans, Green).
1945	*Pledge of Honor, an Albanian Tragedy*, Sami Bey Frasheri; Nelo Drizari, trans. (New York: S. F. Vanni).
1946	*Fairy Tales from Turkey*, Naki Tezel; Margery Kent, trans. (London: Routledge).
1946	*The Star and the Crescent: An Anthology of Modern Turkish Poetry*, Derek Patmore, ed. (London: Constable).
1949	*The Autobiography of a Turkish Girl*, Reşat Nuri Güntekin; Sir Wyndham Deedes, trans. (London: Allen and Unwin).
1950	*Portrait of a Turkish Family*, İrfan Orga (New York: Macmillan).
1951	*Afternoon Sun*, Reşat Nuri Güntekin; Sir Wyndham Deedes, trans. (London: Heinemann).
1952	*Poems*, Nazım Hikmet; Ali Yunus, trans. (Calcutta: Asoke Ghosh).
1953	*Masks or Souls? A Play in Five Acts*, Halide Edib Adıvar (London: Allen and Unwin).
1954	*Poems*, Nazım Hikmet; Ali Yunus, trans. (New York: Masses and Mainstream).
1954	*A Village in Anatolia*, Mahmut Makal; Sir Wyndham Deedes, trans. (London: Valentine, Mitchell).
1955	*Minstrel Tales from Southeastern Turkey*, Wolfram Eberhard (Berkeley: Univ. of California Press).
1955	*Turkish Short Stories*, Halil Davaslıgil and Ayten Davaslıgil, eds. (Ankara: Güzel İstanbul).
1960–61	*Tales of Mullah Nasir-ud-Din*, Eric Daenecke (New York: Exposition).
1961	*Memed, My Hawk*, Yaşar Kemal; Edouard Roditi, trans. (London: Collins Harvill).
1962	*The Wind from the Plain*, Yaşar Kemal; Thilda Kemal, trans. (London: Collins Harvill).

1963   *Turkish Fairy Tales,* Eleanor Brockett (London: Muller).

1963–64   *A History of Theatre and Popular Entertainment in Turkey,* Metin And (Ankara: Forum).

1964   *Tales of the Hoca,* Charles Downing (Oxford, U.K.: Oxford Univ. Press).

1964   *Turkish Fairy Tales,* Selma Ekrem (Princeton, N.J.: Van Nostrand).

1966   *The Exploits of the Incomparable Mulla Nasrudin,* Idries Shah (London: Cape).

1966   *Selected Poems of Yahya Kemal Beyatlı,* S. Behlül Toygar, trans. (Istanbul: Sermet).

1966   *Tales Alive in Turkey,* Warren S. Walker and Ahmet E. Uysal, comps. (Cambridge, Mass.: Harvard Univ. Press).

1967   *Selected Poems,* Nazım Hikmet; Taner Baybars, trans. (London: Cape).

1967   *Watermelons, Walnuts, and the Wisdom of Allah and Other Tales of the Hoca,* Barbara K. Walker, comp. and ed. (New York: Parent Magazine).

1968   *Anatolian Tales,* Yaşar Kemal; Thilda Kemal, trans. (London: Collins Harvill).

1968   *The Pleasantries of the Incredible Mulla Nasrudin,* Idries Shah (London: Cape).

1969   *Fazıl Hüsnü Dağlarca: Selected Poems,* Talat S. Halman, ed. and trans. (Pittsburgh: Univ. of Pittsburgh Press).

1969   *Fifteen Turkish Poets,* S. Behlül Toygar, trans. (Istanbul: İskender).

1969   *Oral Epics of Central Asia,* Norak Chadwick and Victor Zhirmunsky (London: Cambridge Univ. Press).

1970   *The Ballad of Ali of Keshan: An Epic Play,* Haldun Taner, music by Yalçin Tura; Nüvit Özdoğru, trans. (Ankara: International Theatre Institute).

1970   *Hiroshima / Hiroşima,* Fazıl Hüsnü Dağlarca; Talat S. Halman, trans. (Ankara: "Kitap").

1970   *Leylā and Mejnūn,* Fuzuli; Sofi Huri, trans. (London: Allen and Unwin).

1970   *The Moscow Symphony and Other Poems,* Nazım Hikmet; Taner Baybars, trans. (London: Rapp and Whiting).

1971   *I Am Listening to Istanbul: Selected Poems of Orhan Veli Kanık,* Talat S. Halman, trans. (New York: Corinth).

1972   *The Book of Dede Korkut: A Turkish Epic,* Faruk Sümer, Ahmet E. Uysal, and Warren S. Walker, eds. and trans. (Austin: Univ. of Texas Press).

1972	*The Day before Tomorrow: Poems,* Nazım Hikmet; Taner Baybars, trans. (South Hinksey, U.K.: Carcanet).
1972	*The Humanist Poetry of Yunus Emre,* Talat S. Halman, trans. (Istanbul: RCD Cultural Institute).
1972	*The Quatrains of Nesimi, Fourteenth-Century Turkic Hurufi,* Kathleen R. F. Burrill, trans. (The Hague: Mouton).
1972	*The Village in the Turkish Novel and Short Story, 1920–1955,* Carole Rathburn (The Hague: Mouton).
1973	*An Anthology of Turkish Short Stories,* Ali Alparslan, ed. (Istanbul: RCD Cultural Institute).
1973	*They Burn the Thistles,* Yaşar Kemal; Margaret E. Platon, trans. (London: Collins Harvill).
1974	*The Book of Dede Korkut,* Geoffrey Lewis, trans. (Harmondsworth, U.K.: Penguin).
1974	*Iron Earth, Copper Sky,* Yaşar Kemal; Thilda Kemal, trans. (London: Collins Harvill).
1974	*On the Nomad Sea: Selected Poems,* Melih Cevdat Anday; Talat S. Halman and Nermin Menemencioğlu, trans. (New York: Geronimo).
1974	*The Sayings and Doings of Nasrudin the Wise,* Michael Flanders (London: Studio Vista).
1975	*Karagöz: Turkish Shadow Theatre,* Metin And (Istanbul: Dost).
1975	*The Legend of Ararat,* Yaşar Kemal; Thilda Kemal, trans. (London: Collins Harvill).
1975	*Things I Didn't Know I Loved: Selected Poems of Nazım Hikmet,* Randy Blasing and Mutlu Konuk, trans. (New York: Persea).
1976	*The Drum Beats Nightly: The Development of the Turkish Drama as a Vehicle for Social and Political Comment in the Post-Revolutionary Period 1924 to the Present,* Bruce Robson (Tokyo: Centre for East Asian Cultural Studies).
1976	*Gemmo,* Kemal Bilbaşar; Esin B. Rey and Mariana Fitzpatrick, trans. (London: P. Owen).
1976	*An Introduction to Ottoman Poetry,* Walter G. Andrews (Minneapolis: Bibliotheca Islamica).
1976	*The Legend of the Thousand Bulls,* Yaşar Kemal; Thilda Kemal, trans. (London: Collins Harvill).
1976	*Modern Turkish Drama: An Anthology of Plays in Translation,* Talat S. Halman, ed. (Minneapolis: Bibliotheca Islamica).
1977	*The Epic of Sheikh Bedreddin and Other Poems,* Nazım Hikmet; Randy Blasing and Mutlu Konuk, trans. (New York: Persea).

1977	*Hollandalı Dörtlükler / Quatrains of Holland,* Fazıl Hüsnü Dağlarca; Talat S. Halman, trans. (Istanbul: Cem).
1977	*The Turkish Shadow Theater and the Puppet Collection of the L. A. Mayer Memorial Foundation,* Andreas Tietze (Berlin: Mann).
1977	*The Undying Grass,* Yaşar Kemal; Thilda Kemal, trans. (London: Collins Harvill).
1977–2000	*Istanbul Boy: The Autobiography of Aziz Nesin,* part 1: *That's How It Was but Not How It's Going to Be,* part 2: *The Path,* part 3: *The Climb,* part 4: *Middle School Years,* Joseph S. Jacobson, trans. (parts 1–3, Austin: Univ. of Texas Press, 1977, 1979, 1990; part 4, Holladay, Utah: Southmoor, 2000).
1978	*An Anthology of Modern Turkish Short Stories,* Fahir İz, ed. (Minneapolis: Bibliotheca Islamica).
1978	*The Penguin Book of Turkish Verse,* Nermin Menemencioğlu and Fahir İz, eds. (Harmondsworth, U.K.: Penguin).
1979	*The Fish Peri: A Turkish Folktale,* Arrane Dewey (New York: Macmillan).
1979	*Murder in the Ironsmith's Market (The Lords of Akchasaz,* part 1), Yaşar Kemal; Thilda Kemal, trans. (London: Collins).
1979	*Shadows of Love / Les ombres de l'amour,* Talat S. Halman; Louise Gareau-Des Bois, French trans. (Montreal: Editions Bonsecours).
1980	*The Bird and I,* Fazıl Hüsnü Dağlarca; Talat S. Halman, trans. (Merrick, N.Y.: Cross-Cultural Communications).
1980	*Rain One Step Away,* Melih Cevdet Anday; Talat S. Halman and Brian Swann, trans. (Washington, D.C.: Charioteer).
1981	*The Saga of a Seagull,* Yaşar Kemal; Thilda Kemal, trans. (New York: Pantheon).
1981	*Yunus Emre and His Mystical Poetry,* Talat S. Halman, ed. and trans. (Bloomington: Indiana Univ. Turkish Studies; 2d ed., 1989; 3rd ed., 1991).
1982	*Candid Penstrokes: The Lyrics of Me'ālī, An Ottoman Poet of the 16th Century,* Edith Ambros (Berlin: K. Schwarz).
1982	*Contemporary Turkish Literature: Fiction and Poetry,* Talat S. Halman, ed. (New Brunswick, N.J.: Fairleigh Dickinson Univ. Press; London: Associated Univ. Presses).
1982–85	*Türk Şiveleri Lügatı (Divanü Lügâti't Türk),* Kâşgarlı Mahmud; Robert Dankoff and James Kelly, trans. (Duxbury, Mass.: Harvard Univ. Printing Office).
1983	*A Dot on the Map: Selected Stories and Poems,* Sait Faik; Talat S. Halman, ed. (Bloomington: Indiana Univ. Turkish Studies).

1983	*Origins and Development of the Turkish Novel,* Ahmet Ö. Evin (Minneapolis: Bibliotheca Islamica).
1983	*Semantic Structuring in the Modern Turkish Short Story: An Analysis of the Dreams of Abdullah Efendi and Other Short Stories by Ahmet Hamdi Tanpınar,* Sarah Moment Atis (Leiden: Brill).
1983	*Turkish Jokes: Once the Hodja Nasr-ed-Din,* Alice Geer Kelsey, Asian Folklore and Social Life Monographs no. 112 (Taipei: Cultural Service).
1983	*Wisdom of Royal Glory: A Turko-Islamic Mirror for Princes,* Yusuf Khass Hajib; Robert Dankoff, ed. and trans. (Chicago: Univ. of Chicago Press).
1984	*The Early Turkish Novel, 1872–1900,* Robert P. Finn (Istanbul: Isis).
1985	*Poetry's Voice, Society's Song: Ottoman Lyric Poetry,* Walter G. Andrews (Seattle: Univ. of Washington Press).
1985	*Rubaiyat,* Nazım Hikmet; Randy Blasing and Mutlu Konuk, trans. (Providence, R.I.: Copper Beech).
1985	*The Sea-Crossed Fisherman,* Yaşar Kemal; Thilda Kemal, trans. (London: Collins Harvill).
1986	*Nazım Hikmet: Selected Poetry,* Randy Blasing and Mutlu Konuk, trans. (New York: Persea).
1987	*The Birds Have Also Gone,* Yaşar Kemal; Thilda Kemal, trans. (London: Collins Harvill).
1987	*Süleyman the Magnificent Poet: The Sultan's Selected Poems,* Talat S. Halman, ed. and trans. (Istanbul: Dost; rev. ed., Istanbul: BKG, 2010).
1987	*The Wandering Fool: Sufi Poems of a Thirteenth-Century Turkish Dervish,* Yunus Emre; Edouard Roditi and Güzin Dino, trans. (San Francisco: Cadmus Editions).
1988	*Contemporary Turkish Writers: A Critical Bio-Bibliography of Leading Writers in the Turkish Republican Period up to 1980,* Louis Mitler (Bloomington, Ind.: Research Institute for Inner Asian Studies).
1988	*The Prizegiving,* Aysel Özakın; Celia Kerslake, trans. (London: Women's Press).
1988	*The Tales of Nasrettin Hoca,* told by Aziz Nesin; retold in English by Talat S. Halman (Istanbul: Dost).
1988	*Thickhead and Other Stories,* Haldun Taner; Geoffrey Lewis, trans. (London: Forest/UNESCO).
1988	*Twenty Stories by Turkish Women Writers,* Nilüfer Mizanoğlu Reddy, trans. (Bloomington: Indiana Univ. Turkish Studies).

1989	*The Drop That Became the Sea: Lyric Poems,* Yunus Emre; Kabir Helminski and Refik Algan, trans. (Putney, Vt.: Threshold).
1989	*I, Orhan Veli,* Orhan Veli Kanık; Murat Nemet-Nejat, trans. (Brooklyn, N.Y.: Hanging Loose).
1989	*Living Poets of Turkey: An Anthology of Modern Poems,* Talat S. Halman, trans. (Istanbul: Dost).
1989	*Selections from Living Turkish Folktales,* Ahmet Edip Uysal (Ankara: Atatürk Culture Center).
1990	*A Last Lullaby,* Talat S. Halman (Merrick, N.Y.: Cross-Cultural Communications).
1990	*The Pocket Book of Twentieth Century Turkish Poetry,* Yusuf Mardin, trans. and comp. (Ankara: Ministry of Culture).
1990	*Poems of Oktay Rifat,* Richard McKane and Ruth Christie, trans. (London: Anvil).
1990	*A Sad State of Freedom,* Nazım Hikmet; Taner Baybars and Richard McKane, trans. (Warwick, U.K.: Greville Press).
1990	*The Turkish Minstrel Tale Tradition,* Natalie Kononenko Moyle (New York: Garland).
1990	*Unregulated Chicken Butts and Other Stories,* İlyas Halil; Joseph S. Jacobson, trans. (Salt Lake City: Univ. of Utah Press).
1990	*The White Castle,* Orhan Pamuk; Victoria Rowe Holbrook, trans. (Manchester, U.K.: Carcanet).
1990	*Yunus Emre: Selected Poems,* Talat S. Halman, trans. (Ankara: Ministry of Culture; 2d ed., 1993).
1990/1993	*The Art of the Turkish Tale,* 2 vols., Barbara Walker, comp. and ed. (Lubbock: Texas Tech Univ. Press).
1991	*I, Anatolia,* Güngör Dilmen; Talat S. Halman, trans. (Ankara: Ministry of Culture).
1991	*The Intimate Life of an Ottoman Statesman: Melek Ahmed Pasha (1588–1662),* Evliya Çelebi; Robert Dankoff, trans. (Albany: State Univ. of New York Press).
1991	*On the Road to Baghdad: A Picaresque Novel of Magical Adventures, Begged, Borrowed, and Stolen from the Thousand and One Nights,* Güneli Gün (London: Virago).
1991	*The Poet Fuzuli: His Works, Study of His Turkish, Persian and Arabic Divans,* Hamide Demirel (Ankara: Ministry of Culture).
1991	*To Crush the Serpent,* Yaşar Kemal; Thilda Kemal, trans. (London: Collins Harvill).
1991	*Turkish Stories from Four Decades,* Aziz Nesin; Louis Mitler, trans. (Washington, D.C.: Three Continents).

1992	*The City of the Heart: Yunus Emre's Verses of Wisdom and Love,* Süha Faiz, trans. (Dorset, U.K.: Element).
1992	*Modern Turkish Poetry,* Feyyaz Kayacan Fergar, ed. and trans. (additional translations by Richard McKane, Ruth Christie, Talat S. Halman, and Mevlut Ceylan) (Ware, U.K.: Rockingham).
1992	*More Tales Alive in Turkey,* Warren S. Walker and Ahmet E. Uysal, comps. (Lubbock: Texas Tech Univ. Press).
1992	*Please, No Police,* Aras Ören; Teoman Sipahigil, trans. (Austin: Center for Middle Eastern Studies, Univ. of Texas).
1992	*Turkic Oral Epic Poetry: Tradition, Forms, Poetic Structure,* Karl Reichl (New York: Garland).
1992	*Turkish Legends and Folk Poems,* Talat S. Halman (Istanbul: Dost).
1993	*Awakened Dreams: Raji's Journeys with the Mirror Dede,* Ahmet Hilmi; Refik Algan and Camille Helminski, trans. (Putney, Vt.: Threshold).
1993	*Berji Kristin: Tales from the Garbage Hills,* Latife Tekin; Ruth Christie and Saliha Paker, trans. (London: Marion Boyars).
1993	*The Poetry of Can Yücel,* Feyyaz Kayacan Fergar, trans. (Istanbul: Papirüs).
1993	*The Poetry of Yunus Emre, a Turkish Sufi Poet,* Grace Martin Smith, ed. and trans. (Berkeley: Univ. of California Press).
1993	*Short Dramas from Contemporary Turkish Literature,* Suat Karantay, trans. (Istanbul: Bosphorus Univ. Press).
1993	*Voices of Memory: Selected Poems of Oktay Rifat,* Ruth Christie and Richard McKane, trans. (London: Rockingham; Istanbul: Yapı Kredi).
1994	*The Black Book,* Orhan Pamuk; Güneli Gün, trans. (New York: Farrar, Straus and Giroux).
1994	*Nedim and the Poetics of the Ottoman Court: Medieval Inheritance and the Need for Change,* Kemal Silay (Bloomington: Indiana Univ. Turkish Studies).
1994	*Night,* Bilge Karasu; Güneli Gün and Bilge Karasu, trans. (Baton Rouge: Louisiana State Univ. Press).
1994	*Poems of Nazım Hikmet,* Randy Blasing and Mutlu Konuk, trans. (New York: Persea; rev. and exp. ed., 2002).
1994	*The Unreadable Shores of Love: Turkish Modernity and Mystic Romance,* Victoria Rowe Holbrook (Austin: Univ. of Texas Press).
1995	*A Flower Much as Turkey,* Ergin Günçe; Gülay Yurdal Michaels and Richard McKane, trans. (Istanbul: Broy).

1995	*The Song Contest of Turkish Minstrels: Improvised Poetry Sung to Traditional Music,* Yıldıray Erdener (New York: Garland).
1996	*101 Poems by 101 Poets: An Anthology of Turkish Poetry,* Mevlut Ceylan, ed. (Istanbul: Metropolitan Municipality of Istanbul).
1996	*An Anthology of Turkish Literature,* Kemal Silay, ed. (Bloomington: Indiana Univ. Turkish Studies).
1996	*Istanbul Poems,* Mevlut Ceylan, ed. (Istanbul: Metropolitan Municipality of Istanbul).
1996	*Nasreddin Hoca Folk Narratives from Turkey,* Seyfi Karabaş (Ankara: Middle East Technical Univ. Press).
1996	*Poems by Karacaoğlan: A Turkish Bard,* Seyfi Karabaş and Judith Yarnall, trans. (Bloomington: Indiana Univ. Turkish Studies).
1997	*A Blind Cat Black; and, Orthodoxies,* Ece Ayhan; Murat Nemet-Nejat, trans. (Los Angeles: Sun and Moon).
1997	*Curfew,* Adalet Ağaoğlu; John Goulden, trans. (Austin: Univ. of Texas Press).
1997	*Just for the Hell of It: 111 Poems,* Orhan Veli Kanık; Talat S. Halman, trans. (Istanbul: Multilingual).
1997	*The New Life,* Orhan Pamuk; Güneli Gün, trans. (New York: Farrar, Straus and Giroux).
1997	*Ottoman Lyric Poetry: An Anthology,* Walter G. Andrews, Najaat Black, and Mehmet Kalpaklı, eds. (Austin: Univ. of Texas Press).
1997	*Poems,* Cengiz Bektaş (Bloomington: Indiana Univ. Turkish Studies).
1997	*Salman the Solitary,* Yaşar Kemal; Thilda Kemal, trans. (London: Harvill).
1998	*The Poetics of "The Book of Dede Korkut,"* Kamil Veli Nerimanoğlu (Ankara: Atatürk Culture Center).
1998	*Twelfth Song: Translations from the Turkish,* Hulki Aktunç; Leland Bardwell, Cevat Çapan, Günal Çapan, Tony Curtis, Theo Dorgan, Victoria Rowe Holbrook, Orhan Ocak, Nuala Ni Dhomhnaill, Christopher Pilling, and Mark Robinson, trans. (Dublin: Poetry Ireland).
1998	*Water Music,* Lale Müldür; Leland Bardwell, Cevat Çapan, Günal Çapan, Tony Curtis, Theo Dorgan, Victoria Rowe Holbrook, Orhan Ocak, Nuala Ni Dhomhnaill, Christopher Pilling, and Mark Robinson, trans. (Dublin: Poetry Ireland).
1999	*The Drunken Grass and Other Stories,* İlyas Halil; Joseph S. Jacobson, trans. (Holladay, Utah: Southmoor).

1999	*Romantic Communist: The Life and Work of Nazım Hikmet,* Saime Göksu and Edward Timms (New York: St. Martin's Press).
1999	*Shoeshine Ramadan,* İlyas Halil; Joseph S. Jacobson, trans. (Holladay, Utah: Southmoor).
1999	*White Coffee Shop Journal,* İlyas Halil; Joseph S. Jacobson, trans. (Holladay, Utah: Southmoor).
1999	*Yaşar Kemal on His Life and Art,* Eugene Lyons Hébert and Barry Tharaud, trans. (Syracuse, N.Y.: Syracuse Univ. Press).
2000	*Dog Tails,* Aziz Nesin; Joseph S. Jacobson, trans. (Holladay, Utah: Southmoor).
2000	*House of Cards,* İlyas Halil; Joseph S. Jacobson, trans. (Holladay, Utah: Southmoor).
2000	*Mediterranean Waltz,* Buket Uzuner; Pelin Arıner, trans. (Istanbul: Remzi).
2000	*Memoirs of an Exile,* Aziz Nesin; Joseph S. Jacobson, trans. (Holladay, Utah: Southmoor).
2000	*The Other Side of the Mountain,* Erendiz Atasü; Elizabeth Maslen and Erendiz Atasü, trans. (London: Milet).
2000	*A Report from Kulaba,* Fakir Baykurt; Joseph S. Jacobson, trans. (Holladay, Utah: Southmoor).
2000	*A Spring Rain of Four Drops,* İlyas Halil (Saint Laurent, Quebec: Veniard Poets).
2000	*Wanted: Infidel Employees,* İlyas Halil; Joseph S. Jacobson, trans. (Holladay, Utah: Southmoor).
2001	*A Cup of Turkish Coffee,* Buket Uzuner; Pelin Arıner, trans. (London: Milet).
2001	*Dear Shameless Death,* Latife Tekin; Saliha Paker and Mel Kenne, trans. (London: Marion Boyars).
2001	*Dissatisfied,* İlyas Halil; Joseph S. Jacobson, trans. (Holladay, Utah: Southmoor).
2001	*Dog Hunt,* İlyas Halil; Joseph S. Jacobson, trans. (Holladay, Utah: Southmoor).
2001	*Don't Go Back to Kyrenia,* Mehmet Yaşın; Taner Baybars, trans. (London: Middlesex Univ. Press).
2001	*Fourth Company,* Rıfat Ilgaz; Damian Croft, trans. (London: Milet).
2001	*Hayri the Barber: Surnâmé,* Aziz Nesin; Joseph S. Jacobson, trans. (Holladay, Utah: Southmoor).
2001	*Intersections in Turkish Literature: Essays in Honor of James Stewart-Robinson,* Walter Andrews, ed. (Ann Arbor: Univ. of Michigan Press).

2001	*My Name Is Red,* Orhan Pamuk; Erdağ Göknar, trans. (London: Faber and Faber).
2001	*Out of the Way! Socialism's Coming!* Aziz Nesin; Damian Croft, trans. (London: Milet).
2001	*Radical Niyazi Bey,* Muzaffer İzgü; Damian Croft, trans. (London: Milet).
2001	*A Summer Full of Love,* Füruzan; Damian Croft, trans. (London: Milet).
2001	*Temple for Rent,* İlyas Halil; Joseph S. Jacobson, trans. (Holladay, Utah: Southmoor).
2001	*The Time Regulation Institute,* Ahmet Hamdi Tanpınar; Ender Gürol, trans. (Madison, Wisc.: Turko-Tatar).
2001	*Where Are You, Susie Petschek? The Poems of Cevat Çapan,* Michael Hulse and Cevat Çapan, trans. (Todmorden, U.K.: Arc).
2002	*Beyond the Walls: Selected Poems,* Nazım Hikmet; Ruth Christie, Richard McKane, and Talat S. Halman, trans. (London: Anvil, in association with Yapı Kredi).
2002	*Death in Troy,* Bilge Karasu; Aron Aji, trans. (San Francisco: City Lights).
2002	*Human Landscapes from My Country,* Nazım Hikmet; Randy Blasing and Mutlu Konuk, trans. (New York: Persea).
2002	*Laugh or Lament: Selected Short Stories,* Aziz Nesin; Masud Akhtar Shaikh, trans. (Ankara: Ministry of Culture).
2002	*Poems of Nazım Hikmet,* Randy Blasing and Mutlu Konuk, trans. (New York: Persea).
2002	*Socialism Is Coming: Stand Aside,* Aziz Nesin; Joseph S. Jacobson, trans. (Holladay, Utah: Southmoor).
2002	*The Sound of Fishsteps,* Buket Uzuner; Pelin Arıner, trans. (Istanbul: Remzi).
2002	*Stories from the Sandgate,* Jaklin Çelik; Nancy F. Öztürk, trans. (Istanbul: Çitlembik).
2003	*The Garden of Departed Cats,* Bilge Karasu; Aron Aji, trans. (New York: New Directions).
2003	*Gemilé,* Orhan Kemal; Cengiz Lugal, trans. (Istanbul: Anatolia).
2003	*The Idle Years (The Story of a Small Man),* part 2, Orhan Kemal; Cengiz Lugal, trans. (Istanbul: Anatolia).
2003	*The Messenger Boy Murders,* Perihan Mağden; Richard Hamer, trans. (London: Milet).
2003	*My Father's House (The Story of a Small Man),* part 1, Orhan Kemal; Cengiz Lugal, trans. (Istanbul: Anatolia).

2003	*Naked Yula: Stories,* İlyas Halil; Joseph S. Jacobson, trans. (Holladay, Utah: Southmoor).
2003	*The Prisoners,* Orhan Kemal; Cengiz Lugal, trans. (Istanbul: Anatolia).
2003	*Roads and Footprints,* Mustafa Miyasoğlu; Masud Akhtar Shaikh, trans. (Konya, Turkey: Meram Municipal Corporation).
2004	*A Crazy Tree,* Pınar Kür; Ruth Christie, trans. (Istanbul: Epsilon).
2004	*Eda: An Anthology of Contemporary Turkish Poetry,* Murat Nemet-Nejat, ed. (Jersey City, N.J.: Talisman).
2004	*Embracing the Mountains,* Süleyman Sağlam; Nancy F. Öztürk and Adnan Tonguç, trans. (Istanbul: Çitlembik).
2004	*The Flea Palace,* Elif Şafak; Müge Göçek, trans. (London: Marion Boyars).
2004	*The Guests at the Moribund Hotel,* Tomris Uyar; Nilüfer Mizanoğlu Reddy, trans. (Istanbul: Epsilon).
2004	*In the Temple of a Patient God,* Bejan Matur; Ruth Christie, trans. (Todmorden, U.K.: Arc).
2004	*Istanbul Blues,* Buket Uzuner; Pelin Arıner, trans. (Istanbul: Epsilon).
2004	*I've Always Remembered You on Moonlit Nights,* Murathan Mungan; Ruth Christie, trans. (Istanbul: Epsilon).
2004	*The Köşk in Acıbadem,* Ahmet Hamdi Tanpınar; Fatih Özgüven and Victoria Rowe Holbrook, trans. (Istanbul: Epsilon).
2004	*The Long White Cloud: Gallipoli,* Buket Uzuner; Pelin Arıner, trans. (Istanbul: Everest).
2004	*Photo "Sabah" Pictures,* Ayşe Kulin; Martina Keskintepe, trans. (Istanbul: Epsilon).
2004	*The Saint of Incipient Insanities,* Elif Şafak (New York: Farrar, Straus and Giroux).
2004	*Selected Poems,* İlhan Berk; Önder Otçu, ed. (Jersey City, N.J.: Talisman).
2004	*Selected Poems,* Fazıl Hüsnü Dağlarca; Anıl Meriçelli, trans. (Adana, Turkey: Ardıçkuşu).
2004	*Sleeping in the Forest: Stories and Poems,* Sait Faik; Talat S. Halman, ed.; Jayne L. Warner, assoc. ed. (Syracuse, N.Y.: Syracuse Univ. Press).
2004	*Snow,* Orhan Pamuk; Maureen Freely, trans. (London: Faber and Faber).
2004	*Three Stories: Eylül Shall Not Be Here Yet Tomorrow—Eyyup—Sand Coasters up North,* Cemil Kavukçu; İştar Gözaydın, trans. (Istanbul: Epsilon).

2004 *Two Stories: Assimilation—The Door,* İnci Aral; Işılar Kür, trans. (Istanbul: Epsilon).

2004 *An Unprecedented Communal Rite in the Court of Nur Baba,* Yakup Kadri Karaosmanoğlu; Işılar Kür, trans. (Istanbul: Epsilon).

2005 *The Age of Beloveds: Love and the Beloved in Early-Modern Ottoman and European Culture and Society* (with translations of Ottoman poetry), Walter G. Andrews and Mehmet Kalpaklı (Durham, N.C.: Duke Univ. Press).

2005 *Beauty and Love,* Şeyh Galib; Victoria Rowe Holbrook, trans. (New York: Modern Language Association of America).

2005 *Istanbul: Memories and the City,* Orhan Pamuk; Maureen Freely, trans. (New York: Random House).

2005– *Journal of Turkish Literature* (the only English-language scholarly journal devoted in its entirety to Turkish literature), published annually, Talat S. Halman, ed. (Ankara: Bilkent Univ. Center for Turkish Literature).

2005 *Nightingales and Pleasure Gardens: Turkish Love Poems,* Talat S. Halman, ed. and trans.; Jayne L. Warner, assoc. ed. (Syracuse, N.Y.: Syracuse Univ. Press).

2005 *Turkish Delight: An Anthology of Turkish Short Stories,* Masud Akhtar Shaikh, comp. and trans. (Islamabad: Agha Jee).

2005 *Two Girls,* Perihan Mağden; Brendan Freely, trans. (London: Serpent's Tail).

2006 *Ash Divan: Selected Poems,* Enis Batur; Clifford Endres, Saliha Paker, Selhan Savcıgil-Endres, Mel Kenne, Coşkun Yerli, and Ronald Tamplin, trans. (Jersey City, N.J.: Talisman).

2006 *The Bastard of Istanbul,* Elif Şafak (New York: Viking).

2006 *The Black Book,* Orhan Pamuk; Maureen Freely, trans. (London: Faber and Faber).

2006 *Bliss,* Zülfü Livaneli; Çiğdem Aksoy, trans. (New York: St. Martin's Press).

2006 *A Brave New Quest: 100 Modern Turkish Poems,* Talat S. Halman, ed. and trans.; Jayne L. Warner, assoc. ed. (Syracuse, N.Y.: Syracuse Univ. Press).

2006 *Creating a Man,* Necip Fazıl Kısakürek; Masud Akhtar Shaikh, trans. (Islamabad: Agha Jee).

2006 *Early Mystics in Turkish Literature,* Mehmed Fuad [Köprülü]; Gary Leiser and Robert Dankoff, eds. and trans. (London: Routledge).

2006 *The Gaze,* Elif Şafak; Brendan Freeley, trans. (London: Marion Boyars).

2006	*Last Train to Istanbul,* Ayşe Kulin; John W. Baker, trans. (Istanbul: Everest).
2006	*A Leaf about to Fall: Selected Poems,* İlhan Berk; George Messo, trans. (Cambridge, U.K.: Salt).
2006	*The Missing Rose,* Serdar Özkan; Angela Roome and Serdar Özkan, trans. (Istanbul: Timas).
2006	*The Money Games,* Necip Fazıl Kısakürek; Masud Akhtar Shaikh, trans. (Islamabad: Agha Jee).
2006	*Orpheus,* Nazlı Eray; Robert Finn, trans. (Austin: Center for Middle Eastern Studies, Univ. of Texas).
2006	*Saturn: Selected Poems,* Levent Yılmaz; Ünal Aytür, trans. (Riverdale-on-Hudson, N.Y.: Sheep Meadow).
2006	*Tales from the Taurus,* Osman Şahin; Jean Carpenter Efe, ed. (Istanbul: Bosphorus Univ. Press).
2006	*The Turkish Muse: Views and Reviews, 1960s–1990s,* Talat S. Halman; Jayne L. Warner, ed. (Syracuse, N.Y.: Syracuse Univ. Press).
2007	*101 Poems of Nazım Hikmet: A Romantic Revolutionary Turkish Poet,* Masud Akhtar Shaikh, comp. and trans. (Islamabad: Masud).
2007	*Aylin,* Ayşe Kulin; Dara Çolakoğlu, trans. (Istanbul: Remzi).
2007	*The City in Crimson Cloak,* Aslı Erdoğan; Amy Spangler, trans. (New York: Soft Skull).
2007	*Inner Peace,* Ahmet Hamdi Tanpınar; Ender Gürol, trans. (Madison, Wisc.: Turko-Tatar).
2007	*Other Colors: Essays and a Story,* Orhan Pamuk; Maureen Freely, trans. (New York: Alfred A. Knopf).
2007	*Quarreling with God: Mystic Rebel Poems of the Dervishes of Turkey,* Jennifer Ferraro and Latif Bolat, comps. and trans. (Ashland, Ore.: White Cloud).
2007	*Rapture and Revolution: Essays on Turkish Literature,* Talat S. Halman; Jayne L. Warner, ed. (Syracuse, N.Y.: Syracuse Univ. Press).
2007	*Seasons of the Word,* Hilmi Yavuz; Walter G. Andrews, trans. (Syracuse, N.Y.: Syracuse Univ. Press).
2007	*Swords of Ice,* Latife Tekin; Saliha Paker and Mel Kenne, trans. (London: Marion Boyars).
2008	*The Agape Flower,* İlyas Halil; Aimée Murruve, trans. (Ankara: Ürün).
2008	*Autobiographies of Orhan Pamuk: The Writer and His Novels,* Michael McGaha (Salt Lake City: Univ. of Utah Press).
2008	*Face to Face,* Ayşe Kulin; John W. Baker, trans. (Istanbul: Everest).
2008	*Hikâye: Turkish Folk Romance as Performance Art,* İlhan Başgöz (Bloomington, Indiana University Press).

2008	*I, Anatolia and Other Plays: An Anthology of Modern Turkish Drama, Volume 2,* Talat S. Halman and Jayne L. Warner, eds. (Syracuse, N.Y.: Syracuse Univ. Press).
2008	*The Idle Years: My Father's House—The Idle Years,* Orhan Kemal; Cengiz Lugal, trans. (London: Peter Owen).
2008	*In Jail with Nazım Hikmet,* Orhan Kemal; Bengisu Rona, trans. (Istanbul: Anatolia).
2008	*Istanbullu,* Buket Uzuner; Pelin Arıner, trans. (Istanbul: Remzi).
2008	*I've Learned Some Things: Selected Poems,* Ataol Behramoğlu; Walter G. Andrews, trans. (Austin: Univ. of Texas Center for Middle Eastern Studies).
2008	*İbrahim the Mad and Other Plays: An Anthology of Modern Turkish Drama, Volume 1,* Talat S. Halman and Jayne L. Warner, eds. (Syracuse, N.Y.: Syracuse Univ. Press).
2008	*Madrigals,* İlhan Berk; George Messo, trans. (Exeter, U.K.: Shearsman).
2008	*A Mind at Peace,* Ahmet Hamdi Tanpınar; Erdağ Göknar, trans. (Brooklyn, N.Y.: Archipelago).
2008	*The Prophet Murders,* Mehmet Murat Somer; Kenneth Dakan, trans. (London: Serpent's Tail).
2008	*Songs My Mother Never Taught Me,* Selçuk Altun; Ruth Christie and Selçuk Berilgen, trans. (London: Telegram).
2008	*Summer's End,* Adalet Ağaoğlu; Figen Bingül, trans. (Jersey City, N.J.: Talisman).
2008	*Tales of Crossed Destinies: The Modern Turkish Novel in a Comparative Context,* Azade Seyhan (New York: Modern Language Association of America).
2008	*The Turkish Blue: Selected Poems,* Cahit Külebi; Vicki Tuncer and Baran Tuncer, trans. (Ankara: Bilgi).
2008	*Voice of Hope: Turkish Woman Poet Gülten Akın,* Hilal Sürsal (Bloomington: Indiana Univ. Turkish Studies).
2009	*The Book of Madness,* Levent Senyürek; Feyza Howell, trans. (Istanbul: Çitlembik).
2009	*the book of things,* İlhan Berk; George Messo, trans. (London: Salt).
2009	*Essays Interpreting the Writings of Novelist Orhan Pamuk,* Nilgun Anadolu-Okur, ed. (Lewiston, N.Y.: Edwin Mellen).
2009	*Farewell,* Ayşe Kulin; Kenneth J. Dakan, trans. (Istanbul: Everest).
2009	*The Gigolo Murder,* Mehmet Murat Somer; Kenneth Dakan, trans. (London: Serpent's Tail).
2009	*İkinci Yeni: The Turkish Avant-Garde,* George Messo, ed. and trans. (Exeter, U.K.: Shearsman).

2009	*The Kiss Murder,* Mehmet Murat Somer; Kenneth Dakan, trans. (London: Serpent's Tail).
2009	*Many and Many a Year Ago,* Selçuk Altun; Clifford Endres and Selhan Endres, trans. (London: Telegram).
2009	*The Museum of Innocence,* Orhan Pamuk; Maureen Freely, trans. (New York: Alfred A. Knopf).
2009	*Popular Turkish Love Lyrics and Folk Legends,* Talat S. Halman (Syracuse, N.Y.: Syracuse Univ. Press, 2009).
2010	*The Forty Rules of Love,* Elif Şafak (New York: Viking).

INDEX

Cöntürk, Hüseyin, 128
creation, legend of, 5
criticism. *See* literary criticism
Croce, Benedetto, 8
Crusades, 15, 16
Cubism, 100, 113
Cumalı, Necati, 114, 120, 126
Cyrillic alphabet, 1

Çağan, Sermet, 126
Çağlar, Behçet Kemal, 118
Çalıkuşu (*The Autobiography of a Turkish Girl*) (Güntekin), 76
Çamlıbel, Faruk Nafiz, 84, 90, 118
Çapan, Cevat, 115
Çelebi, Asaf Hâlet, 92, 113
Çınarlı, Mehmet, 118
Çiçekoğlu, Feride, 122

Dadaloğlu (19 c.), 27, 29
Dağlarca, Fazıl Hüsnü, 110–13, 118–19, 130–31
Damar, Arif, 114
Dante, 18, 19
Dawn of Freedom (*Fecr-i Âti*) movement, 71, 79
Dayıoğlu, Gülten, 122
"Death of the Epicures" (Beyatlı), 85
Dede Korkut tales (*The Book of Dede Korkut*), 10; Islamic flavor acquired by, 8; in oral tradition, 4; origins of, viii; as Turkish national epic, viii, 8; yearning for peace and tranquility in, 8–9
Dertli (18–19 c.), 29
destan, 27, 57
Devlet Ana (Tahir), 121
Dıranas, Ahmet Muhip, 90, 91
"dig, the" (Yavuz), 103
Dilmen, Güngör, 126
Dinamo, Hasan İzzettin, 121
Divan-ı Hikmet (Ahmet Yesevi), 8

Divan-ı Kebir (Rumi), 13
Divan literature, 34–53; under Abdülhamid, 71; Arabic and Persian influences in, 31, 34–35, 39; auditory imagination in, 40; change resisted in, 50; classification of Ottoman literature, 25; conformism of, 43–44; folk poetry contrasted with, 29; form as supreme in, 35; fresh, compelling metaphors in, 40; as "hermetically sealed" from life, 44; innovations in, 50–53; modernist criticism of, 39–40; mysticism versus orthodoxy in, 47–48; as *poésie pure*, 40; re-Turkification of, 39; on rich versus poor, 44–45; on sacrifice, 67; as satisfying both elite and popular tastes, 31; tyranny opposed in, 45–46; younger poets of Republic on, 84
Divanü Lügâti't Türk (Kâşgarlı Mahmud), viii, 7
Doltaş, Dilek, 129
Doludizgin (Kocagöz), 121
Don Kişot'tan Bugüne Roman (Parla), 129
dramatic literature: in early twenty-first century, 134; of Hikmet, 85; Ottoman, 76–78; tragedy, 31, 78, 126; in Turkish Republic, 125–28; Turks adopt from Europe, 64. *See also* comedy
Durbaş, Refik, 118
Dursun, Tarık, 121
Duru, Orhan, 123

Ecevit, Yıldız, 129
Edgü, Ferit, 116
Edib (Adıvar), Halide, viii, 76, 118
Edib Ahmed (12 c.), 8
efsane, 57
elegies, 6
Elegy to the Cat (Me'âli), 45
50 Yılın Türk Tiyatrosu (And), 126

Süleyman the Magnificent, Sultan, 31,
  42–43, 57
Süreya, Cemal, 107
symbolism, 79, 84, 100, 113

Şafak, Elif, 123–24
Şair Evlenmesi (*The Wedding of the Poet*)
  (Şinasi), 76–77
şarkı (*murabba*), 35
Şems of Tabriz, 12–13
Şemseddin Sami (19 c.), 74, 77
Şener, Sevda, 127
Şenlikname (Berk), 101–2
Şevkengiz (Vehbi), 57
Şeyh Bedreddin Destanı (*The Epic of
  Sheikh Bedreddin*) (Hikmet), 87–90
Şeyh Galib (18 c.), 40, 50–53, 56–57
Şeyhî (15 c.), 36–37
Şeyhülislâm Yahya (16–17 c.), 38, 47
Şeyyad Hamza (13 c.), 26
Şinasi, İbrahim, 59, 64, 65, 67, 76–77
Şirin, Mustafa Ruhi, 122

Tahir, Kemal, 121
tales: essential features of Turkish folk-
  tales, 55; Ottoman, 57–61
Tamer, Ülkü, 116
Taner, Haldun, 123, 126
Tanpınar, Ahmet Hamdi, 90–91, 128
Tanzimat (Reform) Period, 63, 65–66, 71
Tarancı, Cahit Sıtkı, 93
Tarhan, Abdülhak Hâmit, 64, 67–68, 78,
  83–84
Tecer, Ahmet Kutsi, 90, 118
tekerleme, 55, 59
Tekin, Latife, 122
Tekke literature, 25–26
"Terziler Geldiler" (Uyar), 104
Tevfik Fikret, 68–70, 72, 74
tezkire'tüş-şuara, 33

theater: in early twenty-first century, 134;
  Karagöz (shadow play), 25, 31, 58, 126;
  Ottoman, 25; in Turkish Republic,
  125–28. *See also* dramatic literature
Thousand and One Nights, The, 56
"Tiny Spring, A" (Külebi), 93–94
Toprak Ana (Dağlarca), 111, 118–19
Toptaş, Hasan Ali, 122
Topuz, Hıfzı, 121
"To the Fatherland" (Namık Kemal), 66
tragedy, 31, 78, 126
translations, 64
"Troya Önünde Atlar" (Anday), 99
Tulip Age, 50
Turan, Güven, 118
Turkish language: *aruz* as ill-suited to,
  34–35; characteristics of, 3; conti-
  nuity of, 2; Kanık employs natural
  sounds of colloquial, 96; Language
  Revolution, 81; pure Turkish move-
  ment, 81; re-Turkification of, 39;
  Simple Turkish (*türki-i basit*) move-
  ment, 39; Uyghur, vii, 1, 4, 6; vast
  transformation of, 134
Turkish literature: Asian origins of, 1–10;
  cultural and literary orientations in,
  vii; Europeanization of, viii; future
  of, 133–35; geographic span of, vii;
  gulf between elite and popular, 7–8;
  impediments to development of, 134;
  oldest known written, 6; periodiza-
  tion of, 1–2; as premier genre of Turk-
  ish culture, vii, 124; Selçuk, 11–23;
  temporal span of, 1; themes of mod-
  ern, 83; in Turkish Republic, 81–131.
  See also dramatic literature; fiction;
  folk literature; literary criticism; oral
  literature; Ottoman literature; poetry
Turkish Republic, 81–131; establish-
  ment of, 81, 85; future of literature
  in, 133–35; modern literature gains
  ascendency in, viii

Turks: Anatolia conquered by, 9; basic cultural traits of, 1; continuity of Turkish culture, 2; conversion to Islam, 1, 4, 9–10, 56, 57; migration of, 3, 8–9; religions of, 1, 5; scripts used by, 1

Tutunamayanlar (Atay), 122

tuyuğ, 35

Türkali, Vedat, 121

Türkeş, Ömer, 129

türki-i basit (Simple Turkish) movement, 39

türkü, 27

"Two Solitary Trees" (Dıranas), 91

Usûlî (16 c.), 46

Uşaklı, Ömer Bedrettin, 118

Uşaklıgil, Halit Ziya, 75

Uyar, Tomris, 122

Uyar, Turgut, 102–4

Uyghur Turkish language, vii, 1, 4, 6

Uygur, Nermi, 129

Uzuner, Buket, 122

Ümit, Ahmet, 124

vahdet-i vücut, 19–20

Vakaayi-i Acibe ve Havadis-i Kefşger Ahmed, 76

Valéry, Paul, 100

"Vanish" (Cansever), 104–5

varsağı, 27

Vatan yahut Silistre (Namık Kemal), 77

Vehbi (18 c.), 57

verse. *See* poetry

vers libre, 95

Veysî (17 c.), 32

Village in Anatolia, A (*Bizim Köy*) (Makal), 118–19

Village Novel, 119–20

village plays, 126, 127

"Village Without Rain" (Dağlarca), 111, 113

War of Liberation, 110, 118, 121

Wedding of the Poet, The (*Şair Evlenmesi*) (Şinasi), 76–77

Westernization, 63–64, 73, 75, 83

Westöstlicher Divan (Goethe), 11

Whirling (Mevlevi) Dervishes, 12, 15, 26, 51–53

White Castle, The (*Beyaz Kale*) (Pamuk), 125

Wisdom of Royal Glory (*Kutadgu Bilig*) (Yusuf Has Hâcib), viii, 2–3, 7

women: Halide Edib Adıvar, 76, 118; Ottoman poetry by, 48–50

Yağcı, Öner, 122

Yahya of Taşlıca (16 c.), 38, 44

"Yalan" (Anday), 97

Yavuz, Hilmi, 103

Yeni Hayat (*The New Life*) (Pamuk), 125

Yetkin, Suut Kemal, 128

Yirmisekiz Mehmed Çelebi (18 c.), 33

Yorgun Savaşçı (Tahir), 121

Yunus Emre, 16–23; on achieving divinity, 22; on four holy books, 18; on God's revelation in man, 20; humanistic mystic outlook of, viii, 7, 16–17, 20; "International Yunus Emre Year" (1991), 22–23; on love as supreme attribute, 17, 18–19; mystic folk poetry of, 7; naturalism and ecumenism of, 17–18; on orthodox religion, 21–22; Rifat compared with, 97; Rumi's influence on, 16; on service to society, 20–21; stylistic virtues of, 18; Sufi influences on, 18; union with God as theme in, 19; *vahdet-i*

BIOGRAPHICAL NOTES

TALAT S. HALMAN is a critic, a scholar, and a leading translator of Turkish literature into English. His books in English include *Contemporary Turkish Literature, Modern Turkish Drama, Süleyman the Magnificent Poet,* three volumes on Yunus Emre, *Mevlana Celaleddin Rumi and the Whirling Dervishes* (with Metin And), *A Brave New Quest: 100 Modern Turkish Poems, Shadows of Love* (his original poems in English), *A Last Lullaby* (his English/Turkish poems), *Living Poets of Turkey, Popular Turkish Love Lyrics and Folk Legends,* and many books featuring modern Turkish poets (Dağlarca, Kanık, Anday). He is the editor of *A Dot on the Map: Selected Stories and Poems* and *Sleeping in the Forest: Stories and Poems* by Sait Faik. *ForeWord Reviews* named his book *Nightingales and Pleasure Gardens: Turkish Love Poems* one of the ten best university press books of 2005.

Among Halman's books in Turkish are twelve collections of his own poetry (including *Ümit Harmanı,* his collected poems published in 2008), a massive volume of the poetry of ancient civilizations, the complete sonnets of Shakespeare, the poetry of ancient Anatolia and the Near East, Eskimo poems, ancient Egyptian poetry, the *rubai*s of Rumi, the quatrains of Baba Tahir Uryan, two anthologies of modern American poetry, and books of the selected poems of Wallace Stevens and Langston Hughes. Halman was William Faulkner's first Turkish translator; he has also translated Mark Twain and Eugene O'Neill.

Halman has published nearly three thousand articles, essays, and reviews in English and in Turkish. He has served as a columnist for the Turkish dailies *Milliyet, Akşam,* and *Cumhuriyet.* Many of his English articles on Turkish literature have been collected in *Rapture and Revolution: Essays on Turkish Literature.* Selections from Halman's Turkish articles and essays have been collected in two volumes, *Doğrusu* and *Çiçek Dürbünü.* His English reviews of works of Turkish literature have been collected in *The Turkish Muse: Views and Reviews, 1960s–1990s.* Some of his books have been translated into French, German, Hebrew, Persian, Urdu, Hindi, and Japanese. For his work as a translator, he won Columbia University's Thornton Wilder Prize.

His translations of Robinson Jeffers's *Medea,* Jerome Kilty's *Dear Liar* (a play adaptation of the correspondence of George Bernard Shaw and Mrs. Patrick

Campbell), Eugene O'Neill's *The Iceman Cometh,* and Neil Simon's *Lost in Yonkers* were produced in Turkey. *Dear Liar* and *The Iceman Cometh* won best-translation awards. Halman is the coeditor (with Jayne L. Warner) of *İbrahim the Mad and Other Plays: An Anthology of Modern Turkish Drama, Volume 1* and *I, Anatolia and Other Plays: An Anthology of Modern Turkish Drama, Volume 2.*

Talat Halman served as the Republic of Turkey's first minister of culture and later as its ambassador for cultural affairs. He was a member of the UNESCO Executive Board. Between 1953 and 1997, he was on the faculties of Columbia University, Princeton University, the University of Pennsylvania, and New York University (where he was also chairman of the Department of Near Eastern Languages and Literatures). In 1998, he founded the Department of Turkish Literature at Bilkent University, Ankara, and has since been its chairman. He also serves as Bilkent's dean of the Faculty of Humanities and Letters. He is currently serving as president of the Turkish National Committee for UNICEF and editor in chief of the *Journal of Turkish Literature.* Halman is also the general editor of a four-volume history of Turkish literature published in Turkish. Since 2008, he has served as chairman of the board of trustees of the Istanbul Foundation for Culture and Arts, which organizes Istanbul's music, film, and theater festivals and the Biennial of Istanbul.

Halman's honors and awards include many literary prizes, three honorary doctorates, a Rockefeller Fellowship in the Humanities, the Distinguished Service Award of the Turkish Academy of Sciences and of the Turkish Foreign Ministry, the UNESCO Medal, and Knight Grand Cross (GBE), the Most Excellent Order of the British Empire, conferred on him by Queen Elizabeth II.

JAYNE L. WARNER is director of research at the Institute for Aegean Prehistory in Greenwich, Connecticut. She holds a B.A. in classics, an M.A. in ancient history, and, from Bryn Mawr College, a Ph.D. in Near Eastern and Anatolian archaeology. Her publications include *Elmalı-Karataş II: The Early Bronze Age Village of Karataş.* Warner has served as assistant editor of the American School of Classical Studies at Athens and executive director of the Poetry Society of America (New York). She has also served as director of the American Turkish Society (New York) and director of the New York Office of the Board of Trustees of Robert College of Istanbul. She is the editor of *Cultural Horizons: A Festschrift in Honor of Talat S. Halman, The Turkish Muse: Views and Reviews, 1960s–1990s,* and *Rapture and Revolution: Essays on Turkish Literature.* Warner is also associate editor of *Sleeping in the Forest: Stories and Poems* by Sait Faik, *Nightingales and Pleasure Gardens: Turkish Love Poems,* and *A Brave New Quest: 100 Modern Turkish Poems.*